M000015032

# THE
# LITTLE
# BOOK
## OF
# KENT

# THE
# LITTLE
# BOOK
## OF
# KENT

ALEXANDER TULLOCH

The
History
Press

First published 2011
Reprinted 2013, 2015, 2016

The History Press
The Mill, Brimscombe Port
Stroud, Gloucestershire, GL5 2QG
www.thehistorypress.co.uk

British Library Cataloguing in Publication Data.
A catalogue record for this book is available from the British Library.

ISBN 978 0 7524 5834 2

Typesetting and origination by The History Press
Printed in Turkey by Imak.

# CONTENTS

# INTRODUCTION

Kent's position has proven to be both an advantage and a disadvantage, a blessing and a curse. When the rest of the country is experiencing foul English weather, the southern tip of Kent, a mere 21 miles from France, can find itself basking in the warmer climate normally associated with the Continent. The people of Kent can, easily and cheaply, take a quick trip over to France whenever they feel like soaking up some French culture and then return home laden with as much cheese and wine and as many baguettes as they can manage. In fact, many of the people who live in the Folkestone and Dover areas find it is easier, cheaper and far more enjoyable to pop over to France than to travel up to London. There must be few in Liverpool, Birmingham or Edinburgh who do not envy their southern cousins who can get out of bed on a fine summer morning, make their way down to the ferry and, a cup of coffee and a stroll around the deck later, arrive in Calais in time for a splendid Gallic lunch. For those who are really in a hurry and prefer to eschew the more leisurely crossing, there is now the Shuttle. Once all the passport and check-in procedures have been completed, a traveller, with his car-load of passengers, can be on French soil within 35 minutes and driving on (dare I say it?) the wrong side of the road, happily on his way to any destination in Europe or even beyond. And anyone who fancies a spot of Continental shopping but doesn't want to take the car can now jump on a Eurostar train at Ebbsfleet International or Ashford International, indulge in some 'retail therapy' on the *Champs Elysées* and be back home in time to put their feet up and watch *Coronation Street*.

And it works the other way round, too. The towns along and just a few miles inland from the Kent coast frequently enjoy Continental fare at the French, Belgian and even Italian markets that have made their appearance there in recent years. In December, German Christmas markets introduce shoppers in Canterbury's main thoroughfare to the delights of *glühwein*, meaty German sausages (with or without *sauerkraut*), Black Forest cuckoo clocks and skilfully carved wooden toys. And in the background a sound system plays Christmas carols in English and German, adding a Continental flavour to the festive atmosphere and making the whole event a delightful experience. By contrast, the sight of people enjoying their *moules marinières* and bottle of perfectly chilled Sauvignon Blanc on the pavement outside a café on a sunny day in June could hardly fail to make a visitor from Paris or Bordeaux feel very much at home.

All this of course is wonderful but there is another side to the story. The proximity of Continental Europe means that, historically, the county has more than once found itself on the actual or potential invasion frontline. When belligerent 'Johnny Foreigner' on the other side of the Channel took it into his head to visit these isles uninvited with the clear intention of overstaying his welcome, it was Kent that had to prepare for whatever the enemy was preparing to throw at us. Emperor Claudius's Roman legions landed in Kent; the Spanish Armada would have done so in 1588 if the English had not scattered many of their galleons with fire-ships as they lay off the coast at Calais; Napoleon made his (thankfully abortive) plans for invasion between 1803 and 1805 and of course Hitler, had it not been for the brave lads of the RAF, would have sent his divisions rampaging through the orchards of Kent as part of his invasion plan. As it was, the Battle of Britain was fought in the skies above Kent in 1940 and the Luftwaffe was given a bloody nose and sent back to its bases in occupied Europe to reconsider its options. Operation Sea Lion, the Führer's code name for the invasion of Britain, had to be abandoned.

It would be pointless and in fact totally wrong to claim that out of all English counties Kent is unique in having a personality of its own. All areas of the British Isles have characteristics which set them apart from the others: Lancashire is very different from Devon; Yorkshire is certainly not Hampshire and the far North-East in dialect, food and social history is very different from the stock-broker belts of Surrey and Buckinghamshire. But what we can say without fear of serious contradiction is that those aspects of Kent's history, charm and individualism that make it what it is owe a great deal to its contact with the Continent and, in particular, with France.

When he was returning to London after giving the inhabitants of Dover a drubbing, William the Conqueror was confronted by a raggle-taggle army of Kentish peasants and was forced to consider the possibility that another bout of killing and pillaging would perhaps not be the best policy. The stroppy natives agreed to recognise William as their monarch but only if they could retain a certain amount of independence and preserve their age-old customs. William agreed and, according to tradition, the compromise is the origin of the county's motto *Invicta,* (unconquered). And this proud boast is preserved in the symbol of Kent, the prancing untamed white horse, which is thought to have been introduced into Kent by the fifth century Jutish invaders Hengist and Horsa.

## MAN OF KENT OR KENTISH MAN?

There is a long-standing tradition in Kent that everyone born in the county falls into one of two categories. Those born west of the River Medway, running north–south through Maidstone, are known as Kentish Men (or Maids) and those born on the eastern side are Men (or Maids) of Kent. If you were born outside the county, no matter how long you have lived there, you are never more than just a foreigner.

# 1

# A RAMBLE AROUND THE COUNTY

## JUST FOR STARTERS

Kent takes its name from the ancient Britons who occupied the country before the arrival of the Romans. In their Celtic language the word *canto* meant 'edge' (modern Welsh still has *cant* for border or rim) and so presumably they thought of what came to be Kent as the edge of the known world. Julius Caesar, writing in 51 BC, referred to the area as *Cantium*, the home of the *Cantiaci* people. The city of Canterbury takes its name from the same origin and the Coat of Arms for the Kent County Council refers to the county as Cantia.

## THE BASICS

Kent occupies the extreme south-eastern tip of England and is surrounded on three sides by water: to the north by the Thames and the North Sea; to the south-east by the Dover Strait and to the south by the English Channel.

Its length from east to west (maximum) is 65 miles and the distance from north to south at its maximum measures 35 miles. Its total area is 1,442 square miles and it is the tenth largest county in the country.

Kent's population is just under 2 million.

There are more castles in Kent than in any other county in England.

Faversham has just under 500 listed buildings

## SOME ILLUSTRIOUS VISITORS
## & RESIDENTS

**Marcel Duchamp**, the Dadaist artist most renowned for his 'ready-mades', visited Kent twice. His first visit was to Herne Bay in 1913, and his second to Folkestone in 1933 as a member of the French national chess team, but unfortunately he lost most of his games. His performance caused him to say 'not all artists are chess-players, but all chess-players are artists.' The competition was held in the Leas Cliff Hall and the winners were a team from America.

**Wolfgang Amadeus Mozart** visited Bourne Park House near Canterbury in 1765.

**Benjamin Franklin** (1706–90), the American statesman, scientist and general polymath, visited Tenterden in 1783.

**Mahatma Gandhi** visited Canterbury in 1931.

**Queen Victoria** was a frequent visitor to Kent.

**Agatha Christie** was a frequent visitor to The Grand, a hotel on The Leas coastal walk in Folkestone.

**Peter the Great**, Tsar of Russia from 1682 to 1725, had a burning ambition: he wanted to Westernise Russia and as part of his grand plan he set about creating a navy to equal any of those possessed by the European powers of the day.

In May 1698 he turned up at Deptford, then part of Kent, with a huge entourage, intending to study the art of ship-building for himself. He was offered the house of a certain John Evelyn, a noted landowner, gardener and diarist, as accommodation during his sojourn – but John Evelyn lived to rue the day he had been moved by such feelings of welcoming generosity. He had spent a great deal of time, energy and money creating a palatial home with magnificent gardens, but it appears that his royal guests had little respect for other people's property. When they left the house was in a dreadful state; most of the furniture had been destroyed,

*Oast houses such as these are synonymous with Kent and much loved by calendar publishers.*

the carpets had been ruined and the beautiful gardens had been laid waste. At today's value, the cost of repairs was something in the region of £20,000

**King Edward VII** liked Kent and spent a lot of time in Folkestone which he used as a bolt-hole for discreet meetings with his mistress.

**Karl Marx** and **Friedrich Engels,** co-authors of *The Communist Manifesto* (1848), made at least nine visits to Ramsgate.

**Mary Shelley** (1797–1851), the well-known author of the Gothic novel *Frankenstein*, left London in 1832 and took up temporary lodgings in Sandgate near Folkestone. Her stay in the town was occasioned by the outbreak of cholera in the capital.

**Marlon Brando,** Hollywood actor and star of *The Godfather* was a real-life godfather to a boy in the tiny village of Selling near Faversham. The actor visited the village several times in the 1980s as he had fallen in love with the place on an earlier visit.

The writer **H.G. Wells** built and lived in Spade House in Folkestone between 1901 and 1909. It is now an old folks' home. H.G. Wells also has a crater named after him on the dark side of the moon.

**Sir Francis Drake,** renowned for his exploits against the Spanish in the sixteenth century, learned his seamanship in the River Medway. Although a Cornishman by birth, his family lived in Kent for a while and young Francis spent many hours messing about on the river.

The Post-Impressionist painter **van Gogh** taught French at a school in Ramsgate (actually at 6 Royal Road) for a few months in 1876.

**William Willett** (1856–1915), who lived most of his life in Chislehurst, was responsible for dreaming up the idea of British Summer Time. He is commemorated by a sundial set up in his honour in Petts Wood.

**George Orwell** (1903–50) spent time with the hop-pickers near Paddock Wood in 1931. He wanted to experience at first hand the privations of the working man (and woman) during the Great Depression. He was able to draw on his experiences in his novel *The Clergyman's Daughter*.

**John Donne** (1572–1631), leading light among the Metaphysical Poets, was Rector of St Nicholas's Church, Sevenoaks, from 1616 until his death.

The novelist **Joseph Conrad** lived in a house called Oswald's in Bishopsbourne, Canterbury. The house is still standing today. The village hall is called Conrad Hall in the writer's honour.

Then known as Audrey Ruston, the film-star **Audrey Hepburn** lived at Orchard Cottage, Duck Street, Elham near Canterbury

*Audrey Hepburn's temporary Elham home.*

from 1935 to 1940. She attended two schools, one on the village square and the other near Elham Manor. Orchard Cottage can still be seen today, but it has changed its name to Five Bells.

Other erstwhile notable residents of Elham were the former Prime Minister **Anthony Eden** and the actress **Katie Johnson**. She is remembered mainly for her role as Mrs Wilberforce in the Ealing comedy *The Ladykillers*, which also starred Sir Alec Guinness.

## KENTISH CURIOS

The ornately carved wooden desk behind which the President of the United States sits in the Oval Office of the White House has direct links with Kent. The timber used in its construction came from a ship called the *Resolute,* built in Chatham dockyard, after it was decommissioned and broken up in 1879. Even today it is officially referred to as 'the Resolute desk'.

There is a street in Sandwich named 'No Name Street'.

Kent is to get its own Little Mermaid. As part of Folkestone's Triennial Arts Festival in 2011 the harbour will acquire its own version of the famous statue situated just outside Copenhagen harbour.

The TV personality Bob Holness, who was brought up in Ashford, played James Bond several years before Sean Connery. In 1956 he assumed the role in a South African radio adaptation of *Moonraker*.

The tiny but picturesque village of Pluckley is supposed to be the most haunted village in Britain. Depending on who is speaking, the village has between twelve and sixteen spooks that make their appearances at fairly regular intervals.

*Right on Pluckley's village square this fourteenth-century inn is reputedly the most haunted in Kent.*

*Folkestone's cannon ball.*

Pluckley was also the setting for the TV series *The Darling Buds of May* starring David Jason, Pam Ferris and Catherine Zeta-Jones.

The village of Coxheath near Maidstone hosts an annual custard pie-throwing contest in aid of charity. The event was first held in 1967.

There is a cannon ball mounted on a piece of rock in the centre of Folkestone and the accompanying plaque reads: 'This cannon ball, fired by the English during the siege of Boulogne in 1544 has been returned to us by the people of Boulogne as a gesture of the friendship now existing between us.' Interestingly the cannon ball is made of Kent ragstone rather than iron. Ragstone was frequently used to make cannon balls until the reign of Henry VIII.

One of Ashford's claims to fame is that its inhabitants were the first in Britain to see white road markings. The white lines were painted on the Ashford section of the Folkestone–London road in 1914.

The highest temperature ever recorded in Britain was 38.5°C (101.3°F) in Brogdale, a hamlet near Faversham on 10 August 2003.

St Mary's Church on Romney Marsh is the last resting place of E. Nesbit who wrote *The Railway Children*.

Horatia, Lord Nelson's daughter, was married to the vicar of St Mildred's Church, Tenterden.

Maidstone Council's coat of arms features a dinosaur, commemorating the discovery of an iguanodon fossil in a quarry near Maidstone in 1834.

HMS *Victory*, Nelson's flagship at the Battle of Trafalgar (1805) and now permanently exhibited in Portsmouth, was built in Chatham dockyard and launched in 1765. It was also at Chatham that Nelson began his naval career.

Only one of the 'seven oaks' of Sevenoaks survived the great storm of 1987. Strangely, the six that were destroyed by the hurricane-force winds were replaced by seven saplings so that Sevenoaks now has eight!

In 1909 Short Brothers built the world's first aircraft factory at Muswell Manor on the Isle of Sheppey. It was here that John Brabazon, also in 1909, became the first Briton to achieve powered flight. He flew a magnificent 500ft. The Short Brothers factory was moved to Belfast in 1945.

The author Charles Dickens was almost killed in a train crash near Staplehurst on 9 June 1865.

King's School, Canterbury, was founded in AD 597 by St Augustine and is therefore almost 1,000 years older than Eton.

Samuel Plimsoll, who thought of and designed the Plimsoll line, died in Folkestone in 1898.

*St Mary's Church on Romney Marsh.*

Deptford, Greenwich, Woolwich, Lee, Eltham, Charlton, Kidbrooke and Lewisham were all part of Kent until 1889 when they became part of London County. This then, in 1965, became Greater London.

According to Kent folklore when storms lash the coast around Dungeness witches put to sea in eggshells.

The same village features in an old Kentish expression. In the days when unmarried co-habiting couples were said to 'live in sin' they were described in Kent as having 'got married in Finglesham church.' There is no church in Finglesham.

In the village of Finglesham, near Deal, there is a signpost directing travellers to a village and town called respectively Ham and Sandwich.

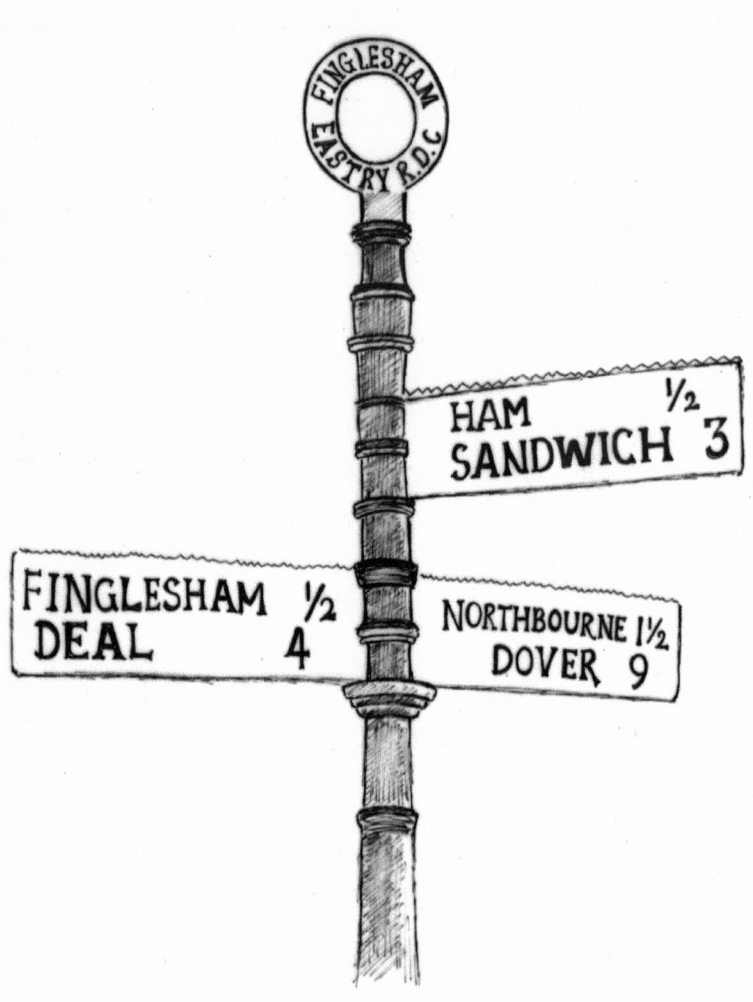

*A signpost for hungry travellers?*

In 1947, when the Romney, Hythe & Dymchurch railway reopened after the Second World War, the ceremonial ribbon was cut by the cinema celebs of the day – none other than Laurel and Hardy.

The nineteenth-century novelist Thomas Hardy was assistant architect to Arthur Blomfield when he designed the building of Dartford Grammar School.

The author Sir William Golding taught at Maidstone Grammar School from 1938 to 1940. In 1970 he was proposed as a candidate for the position of Chancellor of Kent University at Canterbury but was pipped to the post by the Liberal politician Jo Grimond.

Eliot College, part of the University of Kent at Canterbury, was named after T.S. Eliot who died on 4 January 1965, the date of the official opening of the university.

Kent has a nominal border with France under the Channel and half-way through the tunnel.

The medical condition now universally known as OHS (Obesity Hypoventilation Syndrome) used to be called the Pickwickian Syndrome. Patients suffering from this condition have difficulty in breathing when asleep, largely because of their excess weight. The condition was described fully by Dickens in his first novel *Pickwick Papers*, which is set in Kent.

The oldest lych-gate in the country is thought to be that of St George's Church, Beckenham. It dates from the thirteenth century.

Bluewater shopping mall near Dartford attracts more than 27 million shoppers every year. The nearby lakes, however, have nothing to do with the mall's name which is taken from **Blue** Circle, a construction company, and Sheer**water,** a development company.

An old nickname for anyone from Kent was 'Kentish Long-Tail'. The origin of the name was the widely held belief in medieval Europe that all Englishmen had tails.

On Romney Marsh the shepherds are known as 'lookers' and the nineteenth century smugglers were called 'owlers'.

Sir Freddie Laker, the man who introduced cut-price air fares, was born in Canterbury in 1922.

Rochester is one of only three cities in the UK to lose their 'city' status and be demoted back to 'town'. The other two are Perth and Elgin in Scotland.

Dr Richard Beeching, the man responsible for closing down 6,000 miles of rail track in Britain in the 1960s, was born in Sheerness and educated at Maidstone Grammar School.

The stretch of water between Kent and the Continent is known in English as 'The English Channel'. The French call it *La Manche* which literally means 'the sleeve'.

The first international beauty contest was held at the Pier Hippodrome in Folkestone on 14 August 1908. The contest was won by Nellie Jarman, the daughter of a shop-keeper in East Molesey, Surrey. Her prize was a Spencer piano.

Vigo, a village near Gravesend, was formed in 2000 on the site of a disused army camp. It takes its name from a pub on the main road which commemorates the Battle of Vigo Bay, Spain, where the British Admiral George Rooke attacked and plundered the Spanish treasure fleet on 23 October 1702.

There is a plaque in Maidstone town centre which commemorates former mayor Andrew Broughton who, in 1648, read out the death warrant at the execution of King Charles I. The plaque refers to him as 'Mayor and Regicide'.

## SOME ROYAL CONNECTIONS

**Henry VIII** and **Anne Boleyn** spent their honeymoon in Eastchurch near Sheerness.

**Prince Edward, the Duke of Kent,** is currently 27th in line to the throne. He is the Queen's cousin and the grandson of King George V. His appointments include: Chancellor of the University of Surrey; Grand Master of the United Lodge of England and

First Grand Principal of the Supreme Chapter of the Royal Arch Masons of England. He is also 13th in line to the throne of Saxe-Coburg and Gotha.

**Prince Michael of Kent,** the duke's brother, is named after the Grand Duke Michael Alexandrovich Romanov, the younger brother of Tsar Nicholas II of Russia. Prince Michael has always been deeply interested in his Russian ancestry and qualified as a Russian interpreter at the Defence (formerly Army) School of Languages, Beaconsfield, when he was serving in the army. He is also Patron of the Chartered Institute of Linguists.

**Henry IV** (r. 1399–1413) is buried in Canterbury Cathedral. The only other English monarch who is not buried in London is Stephen, the last Norman King of England (r. 1135–41). He died in Dover and is buried in Faversham.

## ROYALS EDUCATED IN KENT

Princess Anne was educated at Benenden School.

Vice-Admiral Tim Laurence was educated at Sevenoaks School.

Diana, Princess of Wales, was educated at West Heath School, Sevenoaks.

## EBBSFLEET OR EBBSFLEET?

Don't confuse Ebbsfleet with Ebbsfleet! If you are travelling to the Continent and want to catch the Eurostar train make sure you go to the right place. There is no station at Ebbsfleet which is situated just south of Ramsgate and is where Hengist and Horsa are supposed to have landed from Germany in the fifth century. For the Eurostar train you have to go to Ebbsfleet International station which is just outside Dartford and approximately 70 miles west of Ebbsfleet.

## KIT'S COTY

Although much smaller in scale, Kent does have its own version of Stonehenge. Just north of Maidstone there is a collection of stones or megaliths dating back to the Neolithic age. Known as Kit's Coty, the site consists of several upright stones topped with a horizontal cap-stone and the whole structure is supposed to be the burial place of the ancient Briton Catigern who, with his brother Vortimer, fought Hengist and Horsa in about the year AD 455. During the battle Catigern and Horsa were killed. We do not know the whereabouts of Horsa's body, but some believe that Catigern's is buried beneath these stones. 'Kit' is taken to be an abbreviation of Catigern and 'coty' is an older, dialect form of 'cote' or 'cottage'.

## KENT IN WARTIME

The very first bomb ever to fall on British soil landed in the garden of a house in Dover on Christmas Eve, 1914. A lone German aeroplane, flown by a Lt von Prondzynski, flew over from France and the pilot lobbed a bomb over the side hoping to hit Dover Castle, probably the most symbolic target on the south coast. The bomb missed the castle by about 400 yards and landed in a private garden. Nobody was killed in the attack but the gardener at St James's Church, who was doing a spot of pruning at the time, was blown off his feet and suffered minor cuts and bruises.

On 27 March 1945 the last V2 rocket fell on English soil. It landed in Orpington killing one woman, Mrs Ivy Millichamp.

Walter Tull, the first black officer in the British Army, was born in Folkestone 28 April 1888. He also played professional football with Tottenham Hotspur and Northampton Town.

Reculver, to the east of Herne Bay, was the site used for testing the Dam Busters' 'bouncing bomb' in the Second World War.

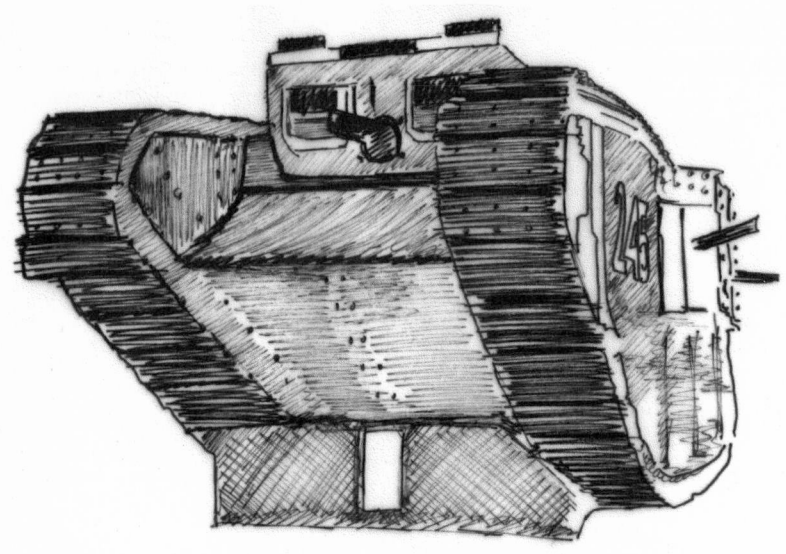

*A First World War tank in Ashford town centre.*

There is a First World War tank on display in the centre of Ashford. It is classed as a 'female' tank because it only has machine guns; 'male' tanks had 6-pounder cannon.

During the First World War a specialist intelligence unit was set up in Folkestone. Under the command of a certain Captain Cecil Cameron it was tasked with processing information brought across the Channel from Holland and Belgium by carrier pigeon.

In 1909 the British Army formed the Kent Cyclists Battalion with its headquarters in Tonbridge. All personnel were trained marksmen and their wartime role was to help defend coastal areas in the event of war. This did not prevent their serving abroad, however, and from March 1916 to November 1919 they served in India.

# ISLE OF THE DEAD?

In a book printed by William Caxton it is suggested that St Augustine drove all the snakes off the Isle of Thanet after he had put a curse on them. From that day forth the isle became a place of death for snakes. The Greek for death is 'thanatos' and this is thought to have given the isle its name

A less fanciful explanation could be that the isle was used as a burial ground by the early inhabitants of Kent. It is known that in Jutish times there were no fewer than six cemeteries on Thanet and so quite possibly the Jutes referred to the place as the isle of 'thanatos' or death

Yet another possibility is that the name has nothing to do with death. It has been suggested that the origin is the Celtic 'teine' (fire) and 'arth' (height) as it was a place used by the ancient Britons for bonfires or beacons.

# MORE KENT TRIVIA

The first ever Ordnance Survey map was begun in 1795 and completed and published in 1801. It was a 1 inch map of Kent.

According to an old tradition it is possible to date fairly precisely the origin of the term 'Garden of England', a title frequently applied to Kent. A certain Richard Harris, Henry VIII's fruiterer, planted a cherry tree near the village of Teynham, just outside Sittingbourne, in 1533 and the county has enjoyed the epithet ever since. In memory of this occasion the civic crest of Sittingbourne bears the image of a cherry tree laden with fruit and the town motto is 'Known by their fruits'.

Old books about Kent will tell you that: 'Cobham churchyard is full of Savages; Northfleet churchyard is full of Badgers; Meopham churchyard is full of Buggs.' The Savages, Badgers and Buggs are the common surnames on the gravestones!

Folkestone boasts a 'water-balance' lift which takes people from The Leas down to the beach. It was built in 1885 and is one of only three in the country.

The mosaic floor in Lullingstone Roman villa dates from the fourth century and contains swastikas in its design.

The Cockney rhyming slang for 'hands' can be either 'Margate sands' or 'Ramsgate sands'.

Former pupils of Sevenoaks School are known as 'Old Sennockians'. However, the apparent connection between the term and the name Sevenoaks is purely coincidental. The Sennockians take their name from Sir William Sennocke, the Mayor of London who founded the school in 1432.

The playwright Samuel Beckett (1906–89), who was living in Paris at the time, crossed the Channel to get married in Folkestone Registry Office in 1961.

There is a hamlet in north Kent called Thong.

The poet and painter Dante Gabriel Rossetti died in Birchington-on-Sea on 9 April 1882 and is buried in All Saints' Church.

The world's biggest offshore wind farm was opened in September 2010 about 7 miles off Foreness Point, near Kingsgate, on the Isle of Thanet.

King George VI had the bright idea of reviving the ancient custom of villages identifying themselves with painted or carved signs and the people of Kent took up the idea with alacrity. Biddenden won a competition for its 'Biddenden Maids' sign in 1920. Now, more than 50 per cent of the villages in Kent have one.

St Ethelburga, (died 647) the daughter of Aethelbert, the first Christian King of Kent, is buried in a church in the village of Lyminge.

*The church of St Mary and St Ethelburga in Lyminge. It was founded as an abbey in AD 633 and is the burial place of St Ethelburga, Queen of Kent.*

## THE BIDDENDEN MAIDS

The village sign at the entrance to the picturesque village of Biddenden, near Maidstone, tells the story of Eliza and Mary Chulkhurst, conjoined twins born in the area in the year 1100. According to this tale the twins were born joined at the shoulder and hip and survived to the age of thirty-four. When one died it was suggested that the surviving sister could perhaps be separated from the deceased but she refused and also died just six hours later.

Whether or not this tale is true is difficult to say. As the twins are not even mentioned in any documents until the eighteenth century some historians maintain that the whole account is nothing more than an entertaining myth.

*Biddenden's maids welcome visitors to the village.*

## VIA FRANCIGENA

Fancy a bit of a stroll? If 1,200 miles is not too off-putting you could follow the 'Via Francigena', the ancient road taken by archbishops from Canterbury when they needed to visit Rome on official business. First mentioned in an Italian document of the ninth century, the route was popularised by Sigeric the Serious (Archbishop of Canterbury, *c.* AD 950–94) who took about twelve weeks to complete the trip on foot, passing through France and Switzerland before entering northern Italy. Modern pilgrims can, and still do, make the journey, having a special passport stamped at Canterbury Cathedral before they set off.

## COURTS OF PIEPOWDER

Queen Elizabeth I granted Maidstone its second charter in 1559 and one of the rights it bestowed on the people of the town was to hold Courts of Piepowder. These were special courts charged with upholding the peace on market days and at fairs and with administering summary justice to those found breaking the law. The term is derived from the Old French *pieds poudrés* (dusty feet), as those who fell foul of these courts tended to be vagabonds and tramps who had walked from so far afield that their shoes were covered with dirt.

## WHOSE TWIN ARE YOU?

| | |
|---|---|
| **Maidstone** | Beauvais, France |
| **Ashford** | Fougères, France |
| | Bad Münstereifel, Germany |
| | Hopewell, USA |
| **Sandgate** | Sangatte, France |
| **Deal** | Saint-Omer, France |
| | Vlissingen, Netherlands |
| **Sandwich** | Honfleur, France |
| **Dover** | Calais, France |
| | Huber Heights, Ohio, USA |
| | Split, Croatia |

| | |
|---|---|
| Ramsgate | Conflans-Sainte-Honorine, France |
| | Chimay, Belgium |
| | Frederikssund, Denmark |
| Margate | Yalta, Ukraine |
| | Idar-Oberstein, Germany |
| Folkestone | Etaples-sur-Mer, France |
| | Boulogne, France |
| | Middelburg, Netherlands |
| Canterbury | Reims, France |
| | Bloomington-Normal, USA |
| Chatham | Valenciennes, France |
| Snodland | Moyeuvre-Grande, France |
| Gillingham | Ito and Yokusuka, both in Japan |
| Dartford | Hanau, Germany |
| | Capelle, Netherlands |
| | Tallinn, Estonia |
| | Namyangju, South Korea |
| Edenbridge | Mont-Saint-Aignan, France |
| Faversham | Hazebrouck, France |
| Royal Tunbridge Wells | Wiesbaden, Germany |
| Sevenoaks | Pontoise, France |
| | Rheinbach, Germany |
| Sittingbourne | Ypres, Belgium |
| Southborough | Lambersart, France |
| Tonbridge | Heusenstamm, Germany |
| | Le Puy-en-Velay, France |
| Gravesend | Neumünster, Germany |
| | Cambrai, France |
| | Chesterfield, USA |
| Broadstairs | Wattignies, France |
| Whitstable | Dainville, France |
| | Borken, Germany |
| | Ričany, Czech Republic |
| | Albertslund, Denmark |
| | Mölndal, Sweden |
| Tenterden | Avallon, France |

## SOME AMERICAN COUSINS . . .

Kent shares its name with the following places in America:
a town in Litchfield County, Connecticut
a city in King County, Washington
a township in Edmunds County, South Dakota
a city in Portage County, Ohio
a town in Putnam County, New York
a township in Dickey County, North Dakota
a city in Wilkin County, Minnesota
a city in Union County, Iowa
a township in Warren County, Indiana
a township in Stephenson County, Illinois

. . . and also

Kent County, Rhode Island
Kent County, Delaware
Kent County, Maryland
Kent County, Texas
Kent County, Michigan
Kent County, Virginia

. . . and the following Kent towns and cities appear in American place names:

**9 Dovers** (in Washington State, Kansas, Illinois, Indiana, two in New Hampshire, New Jersey, Delaware, Florida)

**10 Rochesters** (in Illinois, Indiana, Minnesota, New Hampshire, New York State, Ohio, Pennsylvania, Texas, Vermont, Wisconsin)

**1 Folkestone** (in South Carolina)

**2 Maidstones** (in Vermont and Indiana)

**1 Deal** (in New Jersey)

**3 Canterburys** (in New Hampshire, South Carolina, Florida)

**10 Chathams** (in Massachusetts, New York State, New Jersey, Ohio, two in Illinois, Michigan, Louisiana, Virginia, New Hampshire)

**2 Margates** (in Florida and New Jersey)

## MORE NAMESAKES

The River Kent is nowhere near Kent. It is in Cumbria, about 300 miles to the north-west of the county.

There is another River Kent in Western Australia.

## 007, LICENCE TO KILL

In the 1950s, when the author Ian Fleming was living in Bekesbourne, a village near Canterbury, he needed to decide on a service number for his agent James Bond. Now it just so happened that the bus which ran between Canterbury and London, by way of his village, was the number 007. Several sources suggest that this number sounded just right to him and so the three digits became synonymous with the famous spy throughout the world. And bus number 007 is still the one to catch if you are travelling from Canterbury to London.

Curiously, and presumably entirely coincidentally, the international dialling code for Russia from the UK is also 007. Dear old James (and Ian Fleming) would have been amused.

## HORSMONDEN? WHO'D HAVE THOUGHT IT?

Horsmonden, right in the heart of the Weald of Kent, was once an important centre for the production of artillery. The foundry used to supply the Dutch and English navies with their cannon. It also supplied cannon to Charles I's army and then, during the Civil War, it was the main source of guns for the Parliamentary forces. In 1613 as many as 200 men were employed by the Horsmonden foundry.

Another claim to fame for Horsmonden is that, in 1823, a resident of the village, John Read, invented the stomach pump.

*Horsmonden village sign. Notice the cannon reminding
visitors of the village's military heritage.*

# DISTANCE (BY THE SHORTEST ROUTE) FROM LONDON TO . . .

| | |
|---|---|
| Folkestone | 69.8 miles |
| Dover | 76.4 miles |
| Canterbury | 60.7 miles |
| Ramsgate | 76.7 miles |
| Margate | 75.4 miles |
| Hythe | 67.1 miles |
| Chatham | 32.3 miles |
| Gravesend | 25.8 miles |
| Rochester | 30.8 miles |
| Faversham | 53.2 miles |

# WHAT THE ELL IS AN ULNAGER?

During the Middle Ages one of the most important industries in Kent was weaving and cloth-making. As much of the cloth was produced by small, independent units a certain amount of regulation and standardisation was deemed necessary. The Kentish broadcloth, as it was known, was sold in lengths of between 30 and 34 yards and it had to be 58 inches wide. This width measurement was known as an ell, but things were slightly complicated by the fact that in other parts of the country an ell was 45 inches. It was a measurement mainly used by tailors and was originally based on twice the distance between a man's shoulder to his wrist. The midpoint between shoulder and wrist, the elbow, is a clue to the origin of the term: Latin 'ulna' meant elbow.

In order to make sure that all cloth was sold in accordance with regulation dimensions, officials were appointed to travel around measuring sample cloths with their measuring sticks or 'ellwands'. Such officials were known as 'ulnagers'.

## SOME STRANGE-LOOKING PLACE NAMES IN KENT

**Wrotham:** You would never guess, but the name of this ancient village is simply pronounced 'rootem'. Its origins are somewhat clouded in the mists of time, but there is considerable evidence indicating Roman occupation. Its main claims to fame are that (a) it contains rather a lot of pubs for its size – there are no fewer than three within a hundred yards of each other, and (b) Wrotham transmitting station was the first in the country to use the VHF/FM frequency in 1955.

**Meopham:** Pronounced 'meppem', this village is situated just to the south of Gravesend. The village's Saxon origins can be detected in the history of the name. It was originally Meapaham (Meapa's village) and was first recorded in 788. The former British Prime Minister Sir John Major is Patron of the Meopham Cricket Club and famous residents include the TV personality of the 1950s and '60s Hughie Green (1920–97), the actor Sir Michael Gambon and Kelvin MacKenzie, former editor of the *Sun*.

**Ightham:** You don't even have to be a foreigner to have difficulty with this one! But in fact it is just pronounced as if it were spelled 'item'. The original Saxon name was Ehtaham, meaning 'Ehta's village', Ehta being a Jutish personal name. In 1884 the first sixpenny telegram was sent from the House of Commons to one Joshua Durling, the Ightham postmaster.

Very close to the village is **Ightham Mote**, a manor house dating from about 1320. The 'mote' element of the name indicates that it was used as a meeting place where legal, commercial and civil matters were discussed. 'Mote' is Anglo-Saxon for meeting but later came to mean anything that was discussed at such meetings. Hence in modern English a 'moot point' (different spelling but the same word) is just a matter which needs to be discussed.

**Hoo:** With this one what you see is what you say. The Hoo Peninsula takes its name from the Anglo-Saxon word for a 'ridge' or 'spur of land' and is a bleak, flat marshland on the north coast of Kent. It is probably most famous for being the backdrop to the opening scenes of the Dickens novel *Great Expectations*.

The area around Cliffe, a village on the Hoo Peninsula, doubled as the paddy-fields of Vietnam in Stanley Kubrick's 1987 film *Full Metal Jacket*.

**Lympne:** A picturesque village just outside Folkestone, the name is pronounced exactly the same as 'limb'. The Roman name for it was Port Lemanis and this in turn was a borrowing from a former Celtic name meaning River of Elms. Its tiny airport's claim to fame is that it was the take-off place for Amy Johnson's solo flight to Cape Town in 1932. Another female solo flyer, Jean Batten, also flew from Lympne in 1934 when she beat Amy Johnson's distance record by flying to Darwin, Australia.

**Sandwich:** People who are unfamiliar with the geography of Kent look at this word and immediately think of some edible delicacy served up between two slices of bread. But there is a direct connection between the town in Kent and the portable snack. The story goes that John Montagu, 4th Earl of Sandwich, was an *aficionado* of the gaming tables and one night ordered his valet to prepare him a meal which would allow him to eat without breaking off from his game of cards. An alternative account is that the earl was in fact a conscientious First Lord of the Admiralty and the sandwich (the original one is thought to have been a slice of salt beef between two slices of toasted bread) allowed him to eat while working at his desk.

**Old Wives Lees:** Situated on a high point in the North Downs among orchards and hop gardens this little village enjoys one of the most beautiful positions in the whole of Kent. Nobody has come up with a satisfactory explanation for the origin of the name and all that seems certain is that it was originally Oldwood's Lees, after John Oldwood who owned a manor house nearby in the fifteenth century. The Mount, the highest point in the village, featured in the shooting of the film *Last Orders* (2000) starring Bob Hoskins and Michael Caine.

## YOU'VE SEEN THEM ON TV

| | | |
|---|---|---|
| Gloria Hunniford | lives in | Sevenoaks |
| Michael Bentine | grew up in | Folkestone |
| Tony Hart | was born in | Maidstone |
| Bob Holness | grew up in | Ashford |
| Rod Hull | was born on | the Isle of Sheppey |
| | | |
| David Starkey | lives in | Barham |
| Michael Hogben | was born in | Folkestone |
| Jilly Goolden | was educated in | Tonbridge |
| Ian Hislop | lives in | Sissinghurst |
| Paul O'Grady | owns a farm in | Aldington |
| Julian Clary | lives near | Ashford |
| Tracy Emin | was brought up in | Margate |
| Carol McGiffin | was born in | Maidstone |
| Kate Bush | was born in | Bexleyheath |
| Sir Henry Cooper | lived in | Hildenborough |
| Sir David Frost | was born in | Tenterden |
| Antony Worrall Thompson | was educated in | Canterbury |
| Peter Sissons | lives in | Sevenoaks |
| Fiona Phillips | was born in | Canterbury |
| Joanna Lumley | lived at | Goodnestone |
| Gary Rhodes | studied at | Thanet College |
| Bob Monkhouse | was born in | Beckenham |
| Len Goodman | opened his first dance school in | Dartford |

# 2

# HISTORIC KENT

## HISTORY AT A GLANCE
## – A KENT TIMELINE

| | |
|---|---|
| **55–54 BC** | Julius Caesar invades Britain, landing on the Kent coast |
| **AD 43** | Claudius invades Britain. First Roman fort built at Canterbury |
| **130** | Lighthouses built at Dover |
| **270–90** | Walls built around Canterbury |
| **449** | According to legend Hengist and Horsa come to defend Kent |
| **597** | Augustine arrives in Kent. Bishopric established in Canterbury |
| **774** | Kent rebels against King Offa of Mercia |
| **797** | First Danish and Viking invasions |
| **851** | King Athelstan defeats the Vikings at Sandwich |
| **893** | Viking fort built at Appledore |
| **1011** | Canterbury besieged by Vikings |
| **1082** | Odo, Earl of Kent, banished |
| **1147** | Benedictine Abbey founded at Faversham |
| **1155–6** | Charters give rights to the Cinque Ports |
| **1170** | Archbishop Thomas Becket murdered in Canterbury Cathedral |
| **1215** | Rochester castle besieged |
| **1217** | Sea battle off Sandwich against the French |
| **1290** | Edward I constructs a castle at Sandwich |
| **1348–9** | The Black Death kills almost half the population of Kent |
| **1381** | Peasants' Revolt takes place |
| **1448** | Canterbury is granted a charter |

| | |
|---|---|
| **1450** | Jack Cade leads a revolt in Kent |
| **1452** | John Wilkins leads rebellion |
| **1457** | Sandwich is sacked by the French |
| **1539–44** | Henry VIII constructs castles, many of them in Kent |
| **1548** | Charter granted to Maidstone |
| **1554** | Wyatt Rebellion in Kent |
| **1560–80** | Refugees from the Low Countries settle in Sandwich and Canterbury |
| **1588** | Kent prepares for invasion by the Spanish Armada |
| **1642** | The Civil War starts and Kent stays mainly Royalist |
| **1647** | Cromwell bans Christmas, causing riots in Canterbury |
| **1648** | Battle of Maidstone takes place |
| **1660** | Restoration of the Monarchy. Charles II lands in Dover |
| **1665** | First Royal Navy dockyard constructed at Sheerness |
| **1667** | Dutch fleet enters the Medway and the Thames |
| **1717** | The first newspaper (the *Kentish Post*) for Kent is published |
| **1720–5** | Mereworth Castle built near Maidstone |
| **1758** | Defence systems known as the Chatham Lines built |
| **1796** | Early warning semaphore stations established across Kent |
| **1805–9** | Military Canal constructed as defence against Napoleon. System of seventy-four Martello Towers built along south coast |
| **1810** | Folkestone harbour constructed |
| **1815** | Steamboats begin operating between London and Margate |
| **1823** | Cobbett publishes account of his rides through Kent |
| **1830** | The Swing Riots begin |
| **1835** | First oasthouse with its conical shape built by John Reid |
| **1842–3** | South-Eastern railway line laid |
| **1844** | Faversham connected to the railway system |
| **1847** | Gunpowder factory explodes in Faversham – fifty people killed |

| | |
|---|---|
| **1857** | Formation of Kent County Constabulary |
| **1859** | Kent County Cricket club established |
| **1889** | Kent County Council formed |
| **1896** | Over 100 die in outbreak of typhoid in Maidstone |
| **1909** | Louis Blériot completes historic flight from Calais to Dover |
| **1913** | Kent coalfield opens |
| **1914** | HMS *Bulwark* explodes in the Medway leaving 800 dead |
| **1916** | Explosion in munitions factory in Faversham – over 100 killed |
| **1940** | Kent involved in evacuation of troops from Dunkirk |
| **1942** | Canterbury bombed during so-called Baedecker raids |
| **1944** | 'Doodlebugs' and V2 rockets fall in Kent |
| **1945** | End of Second World War celebrations throughout Kent |
| **1953** | Many coastal towns in Kent affected by serious floods |
| **1960** | Closure of Royal Dockyard at Sheerness |
| **1964** | Nuclear power station opened at Dungeness |
| **1981** | Closure of Royal Naval Dockyard, Chatham |
| **1989** | Ten marines killed by IRA bomb in Deal |
| **1972** | Local government boundary changes in Kent |
| **1976** | Opening of the Dartford tunnel linking Kent with Essex |
| **1989** | Closure of last colliery in Kent |
| **1991** | Opening of Queen Elizabeth II Thames bridge |
| **1994** | Channel Tunnel opens |
| **1996** | Serious fire inside the Channel Tunnel |
| **2000** | Fifty-eight illegal immigrants found dead inside lorry landing at Dover |
| **2003** | Rowan Williams becomes 104th Archbishop of Canterbury |
| **2006** | Securitas Depot robbery |
| **2011** | *The Spirit of Britain*, the largest ferry ever to operate between Dover and Calais launched |

# HOW IT ALL BEGAN

*55–54 BC*

This is probably one of the most important dates in the history of Britain as a whole, but it was Kent that bore the brunt of Roman legions' thrust from their bases in Gaul (modern France). According to Caesar's own account, he and two legions (approximantely 10,000 men) suddenly appeared around Dover in August 55 BC but he was somewhat discouraged when he saw the height of the cliffs (known to us as the White Cliffs of Dover) and the hordes of ancient Britons (who would, more accurately, have been members of the Cantiaci tribe) waving their spears and threatening to do unspeakable things to any Roman soldier who dared to set foot on the shore.

Discouraged, but not deterred, Caesar gave orders for his men to sail up the coast a bit to the gently sloping shoreline around modern Walmer and Deal. Legend has it that even here his soldiers were less than eager for the fight and that it took one brave standard-bearer to leap into the water and call to his comrades-in-arms to follow his example. Fortunately for Caesar his men did finally jump down from their ships and were able to secure a bridgehead on land. When the ancient Britons, who had been observing their progress around the coast, turned up to engage the Roman soldiers in mortal combat, it turned out that they might have been barbarians, but they knew how to put up a good fight. Moreover, they still made skilful use of the battle chariots which the Romans had long since discarded as engines of war and so were able to cut down many of the invaders before they had even scrambled off the beach. Eventually, however, the superior tactics of Caesar's men held sway and the soldiers of Kent were beaten back. Victory, albeit a Pyrrhic one, went to the Romans and the ancient Britons were forced to accept defeat. What Caesar had not taken account of in his preparations for invasion, however, was the weather, and no sooner had he gained his victory than a dreadful storm lashed his ships and many of them were dashed to pieces on the beach. Consequently, he did not have sufficient ships to transport cavalry from the other side of the water to help him strengthen his toehold on Kent, and he was forced to return to Gaul.

He returned the following year with a far stronger force of five legions (about 25,000 men), but unbelievably many of his ships were wrecked again in another storm just off the coast at Deal. This allowed the native Britons time to regroup under their leader Cassivellaunus. He led a very effective guerrilla war against the forces of Rome and might have enjoyed considerable, if not total success in driving them back into the sea, but he was betrayed and Caesar gained the victory he so desperately wanted. However, rebellious tribes in Gaul forced him to return to the Continent and he never came to Kent or Britain again. Nevertheless he had done his duty as a soldier of Rome and begun the process which was taken up again in AD 43. This time the emperor Claudius sent Aulus Plautius with an army of approximately 40,000 men to finish off the job. Sailing from Gesoriacum (modern Boulogne), Plautius set a course for Richborough, near the Isle of Thanet, which in those days was situated on the coast. His landing was virtually unopposed and such opposition as existed was half-hearted and badly organised. The few Britons who put up a fight were chased as far inland as London and the Roman occupation of Britain had begun.

# THE DEPARTURE OF THE ROMANS AND THE AFTERMATH

## AD 449

When the Romans were forced to withdraw from Britain to defend their Empire on the Continent, which was under ever-increasing attacks from barbarian tribes, a power vacuum was left. Eventually, however, the independent Kingdom of Kent was established in 449 with its main towns Dover, Canterbury and Rochester. It has to be said at this point that accounts do vary (in some places they actually contradict each other) but the bones of the truth seems to be the following. The first recorded King was Hengist (449–88) who, with his brother Horsa, had been invited by Vortigern to come over from their native Jutland to help stave off attacks from the Scots and Picts. In return they were given the whole of the Isle of Thanet (which was a real island in those days) for services rendered. After a while the Jutish brothers got a bit greedy and demanded more of the surrounding land and this led to conflict and outright war with their former hosts. The native Britons did put up a fight but were outclassed by the superior fighting prowess of the invaders and suffered particularly humiliating defeats at the Battle of Aylesford and Creganford (modern Crayford). But for some reason, which has never been satisfactorily explained, their leader Vortigern was allowed to remain their king and some attempt at peaceful co-existence was attempted although the 'armistice' appears to have been nothing more than a cunning ruse. In 460 a banquet was proposed to celebrate the advent of peace but, according to the historiographer Geoffrey of Monmouth, the Britons attended the feast unarmed only to be met by heavily armed Jutes who then set about slaughtering them. Vortigern managed to escape and muster enough supporters to engage his enemies again, this time at the Battle of Wippedesfleot (modern Ebbsfleet), but yet again had to flee the field of battle having been thoroughly routed by Hengist.

The cold-blooded murder of the Britons attending what they thought was going to be a celebratory feast introduced a new expression into English. Geoffrey of Monmouth described the affair as 'The Night of the Long Knives'. This was the first use of a phrase which has entered into the language to describe almost any act of treacherous removal of one's opponents.

There is some scriptural evidence of another battle being fought in 473 at a place which is yet to be identified and this time the Britons were utterly routed and certainly did not live to fight another day. No further mention is made of Hengist in the annals and all we know for sure is that his son, Aesc, (or Oisc) became king of Kent in 488 and ruled for the next forty years.

Kent's independence came to an abrupt end in AD 686. Caedwalla, King of Wessex, decided to do a spot of empire-building and invaded Kent, installing his brother Mul on the throne. This did not go down well with the boys from Kent and so they rebelled and killed the impostor. This so infuriated Caedwalla that he returned to make a thorough job of devastating Kent. After a period of anarchy, Oswine (a client king of the Mercians), took control but only managed to reign for about two years. At this point the throne was taken over by Wihtred who seems to have been reasonably successful at restoring order. In 694 he and the West Saxons came to an agreement when he agreed to pay some sort of compensation for the killing of Mul.

When Wihtred died in 725 Kent slipped once more into a state of disorder. Various people attempted to establish the rule of law but without much success and the consequent fragmentation meant that the county was ripe for occupation. It is hardly surprising, then, that Offa, King of Mercia, should seize control in 764 and rule it with a succession of client (or 'puppet') kings. By about 770 he decided he would have to take direct control but (and historical record is not clear-cut here) his attempts appear to have been less than totally successful and were met with another rebellion. It seems safe to assume that the people of Kent sent Offa packing at this point although he did come back and re-establish his rule in 785. When Offa died in 796 there was another period of see-saw victory and defeat for a series of would-be rulers, but eventually it ceased to be an independent county and became part of Wessex in 825. Under Alfred the Great this was the only English kingdom to offer serious resistance to the Viking invaders and it was Alfred's successors who united all England as a single monarchy by 954. Kent was no longer an independent or even a semi-independent kingdom.

## THE KINGS OF KENT (DATES CERTAIN)

| | |
|---|---|
| Aethelbert | 560–616 |
| Eadbald | 616–40 |
| Earconbert | 640–64 |
| Ecgbert | 664–73 |
| Hlothere | 673–85 |
| Eadric | 685–6 |

(at this point there is a gap in our knowledge)

| | |
|---|---|
| Wihtred | 694–725 |
| Eadbert | 725–48 |
| Aethelbert | 748–62 |

(now there was a period of joint kingship, but the names are lost to us)

| | |
|---|---|
| Eadbert | 796–8 |
| Cuthred | 798–805 |
| Baldred | 805–23 |
| Ecgbert (and of Essex) | 825 |
| Aethelwulf (and of Essex) | 825–39 |
| Aethelstan | 839–50 |
| Aethelwulf (again) | 856–8 |
| Aethelbert | 858–60 |

## ALFRED TO THE RESCUE!

*851*

It is probably just as well that Kent was subsumed into the greater alliance of Wessex otherwise the history of the region could have been very different. Alfred, King of Wessex (generally known as Alfred the Great), came to the rescue on more than one occasion when the Viking invasions started. While vast tracts of England were being overrun by Vikings, and in particular the Danes, Kent suffered attacks but never became part of what we now refer to as the Danelaw. In 851 a Viking army sailed up the Thames and then turned on Canterbury, no doubt attracted by the thought of the ecclesiastical treasures in its vaults lying there just ripe for the taking, and sacked it. Simultaneously they occupied the old Anglo-Saxon settlement at Appledore, some 30 miles away. Details are sketchy about how long they stayed but we do know that they laid waste to Canterbury and accounts of the time speak of three successive years of life being difficult under the yoke of the 'heathen army'. What we do know, however, is that Alfred turned up with his army and routed the Danes.

Rochester was another site of great importance for the religious life of Kent. In fact, at that time it was the only city apart from Canterbury in the whole country that had a cathedral, but it differed from Canterbury in that it had robust and virtually impenetrable defences so that the citizens were able, in 855, to hold out against a Viking onslaught until Alfred, once again, arrived and drove the invaders away.

The people of Kent suffered terribly at the hands of the Vikings, but it could have been a lot worse. Alfred's intervention saved the county from permanent occupation and his insistence on drastic measures being taken to ensure the future security of his kingdom meant that by the end of the ninth century the Danish raids on Kent ceased.

## ... AND ALL THAT

### 1066

This is probably the most famous date in the whole of English history. It must be well-nigh impossible to find anyone in the country who does not know that this was the year when the Duke of Normandy, otherwise known as William the Conqueror, defeated Harold at the Battle of Hastings. What is perhaps not so well known is that the Norman Conquest was not a uniform invasion; there are some parts of England where resistance to the all-conquering duke was greater than in others and, as legend has it, Kent offered stiffer opposition than most. In fact, if the historical accounts of what actually happened are true, Kent was never conquered but came to what might be described as a convenient accommodation with the enemy.

After defeating Harold's army William turned his attention eastwards. His men had been given a hot reception the previous year when he had attempted to land an army at Romney and he was determined to be avenged. He all but totally destroyed the tiny Kent town and then set off to take Dover. This he did in a particularly savage manner. First he seized the castle and, *pour encourager les autres,* had the governor beheaded in public. His next move was to turn his unruly troops loose on the town where they indulged in an orgy of rape and pillage. At some point, however, William realised that he had perhaps gone too far. After all, he needed Dover and the men of Dover to be on his side if he was going to defend his newly conquered lands against possible invasion from outside. He therefore withdrew his men and headed back to London where, in an act of humiliation for the

Anglo-Saxons, he crowned himself (quite literally: he put the crown on his head with his own hands) on Christmas Day 1066. He must have thought that he was home and dry. Any opposition to his reign would simply be a matter of a few 'mopping up' operations and then he set about putting his mark on the English and turning it into a vassal state of Normandy. But things were not quite so easy.

One of the first things he had to do after his coronation was head back to Dover in order to secure the castle. No commander could fail to realise that Dover was the 'key to the kingdom', and that if the men of Kent chose not to cooperate with whoever was in power in London, the country could be made almost ungovernable. At this point the border separating myth from the truth becomes a little fuzzy, but the most commonly repeated description of what happened next comes to us from William Lambarde's *Perambulation of Kent* (1570). According to his account the people of Kent were more than just a shade displeased with the treatment the Normans had been doling out to them since the conquest. A group of them gathered together at Swanscombe near Gravesend where Stigande, Archbishop of Canterbury, and Egelsine, the Abbot of St Augustine's, were elected leaders and spokesmen for the imminent confrontation with William. It was at this confrontation that the men of Kent offered the duke a choice between war and obedience based on mutual respect and co-operation. If he chose the latter the men of Kent demanded to be allowed to preserve their own traditions and ancient liberties and, faced with an offer he could not refuse, William agreed. Technically, therefore, Kent was never conquered but entered into a kind of federal alliance with the rest of the country and, so legend has it, became the 'invicta' (unconquered) county. As a result Kent became officially a County Palatine (i.e. governed by a hereditary nobleman but enjoying a degree of independence from the rest of the country) and was administered by William's half-brother Odo, Bishop of Bayeux.

One of the traditions which the people of Kent were allowed to retain was the system of inheritance known as 'gavelkind'. This meant that when a man died intestate his property and possessions were divided up equally among all his sons. In the rest of the country William enforced the Norman system known as 'primogeniture' whereby the eldest son inherited everything. Gavelkind was not abolished until 1925 when the Law of Property Act came into force.

Another of the 'ancient liberties' which survived the Norman invasion was the survival in Kent of the administrative unit known as the 'lathe'. This is almost certainly a hang-over from the Jutes who divided the county in 'lathes', mainly for judicial purposes. The Domesday Book (1086) tells us that Kent was divided into seven lathes: Aylesford, Milton, Sutton, Borough, Eastry, Lympne and Wye. These old Jutish land divisions remained in force for taxation purposes until the seventeenth century, although as early as 1295 they had been reduced to five: Borough and Eastry were combined to form the Lathe of St Augustine; Lympne was renamed Shepway and Sutton, Milton and Wye were combined and then split up again into the Lathes of Scraye and Sutton-at-Hone.

Each lathe was further divided into so many 'hundreds' which in turn were sub-divided into parishes grouped together and centred on a court or similar meeting place where people could gather to discuss the routine business and legal matters of the day.

In addition to the lathe there was another land measurement, of Jutish origin, and used only in Kent. This was the *sulung* and is thought to have covered approximately 160 acres.

# 3

# KENT'S CASTLES

## DOVER CASTLE

William the Conqueror had been on the throne of England for only a matter of weeks when he travelled down to Dover to inspect the castle. The defeated Harold had recently completed a certain amount of renovation and strengthening of the defences but they were not good enough for William and he had his own ideas of what a castle should be. It the first place, it had to be imposing and strong enough to make any future invader think twice, but also it had to be a visible reminder to the local populace that they had a new king. William had come to an understanding with the people of Kent, but he still needed a symbol of his ultimate authority and a virtually impenetrable castle in a prominent position was exactly that.

Dover Castle is probably the oldest castle in the whole of Britain. It is known that a primitive defensive construction was built on the site as far back in history as the Iron Age. We know also that the Romans built a lighthouse (known as a 'pharos') in the same place in the first century and we can safely assume that rudimentary defence workings were built around it. Then the Anglo-Saxons developed it in the tenth century and laid the foundation to what was to emerge as a fortified town. The greater part of the castle, however, is Norman, but most of what a visitor sees there today dates from the twelfth century or even later.

At some time in the 1180s Henry II ordered the building of the great keep or tower and the inner courtyard or bailey dates from around the same time. Most of the remaining part was built by Hubert de Burgh who was constable of the castle between 1202 and 1232.

From the Middle Ages onwards there was a fairly protracted period when the castle fell into a state of semi-disrepair and no further additions were made, although it did not lose any of its significance as a bulwark against possible invasion. In the eighteenth century the authorities had another look at the place and decided that a few changes were necessary. New barracks were built and major reconstruction and strengthening of the outer defences was undertaken. Some of the towers were dismantled or at least lowered to make way for modern artillery positions.

In response to the threat of invasion in Napoleonic times, a vast network of tunnels was dug beneath the castle and into the actual rock face. Although their construction proved to be somewhat premature and were never used in the defence of this country against Napoleon, they did come into their own during the Second World War. The whole underground warren proved an excellent bomb-proof command post for maritime operations and served as the base from which the evacuation of Dunkirk (1940) was coordinated.

It might seem unbelievable, but the building which largely took shape under the watchful eyes of the Duke of Normandy in the eleventh century did not cease to have a military role until the 1980s. During the Cold War there were plans to reactivate Dover Castle in the event of nuclear war and use it as a base for both military personnel and regional government.

## LEEDS CASTLE

Dover might be the largest and strategically most important castle in the land but there is little room for discussion when it comes to choosing the most beautiful: Leeds has to be the winner by a mile. The castle takes its name from Ledian who was presented with the original manor house by Aethelbert, the ninth-century King of Kent, for services rendered.

Situated about 40 miles inland from its coastal rival it stands in the middle of 500 acres on three islands in the middle of a lake and is surrounded by some of the most beautiful gardens in Kent. And once again, the man we have to thank for leaving us such a wonderful legacy is none other than William the Conqueror. It had been little more than a Saxon timber palisade when William decided to enlarge it and then the job was finished off in the thirteenth century when Edward I (r. 1272–1307) and his queen, Eleanor of Castile, turned it into a stone fortress. Perhaps its greatest claim to fame, however, is that it is the cradle of the Tudor dynasty. Catherine de Valois (the Dowager Queen) began an affair here with a courtier called Owen Tudor and Henry VII, the first Tudor King, was their grandson.

Then just as the fashion for blockbuster castles was on the decline, Henry VIII came along in the sixteenth century and, enamoured of the castle's position and design, decided to beautify it a little and convert it into a royal palace in honour of his first wife, Catherine of Aragón. However, Henry's conversion of the castle into a palace did not involve the sacrifice of its military significance. It still represented a royal powerbase and it maintained a substantial contingent of men-at-arms for the defence of the monarchy and as a military fortification to be used in the event of an attack by French or Spanish forces. He also made use of Leeds Castle as a bolt-hole when he wanted to escape the outbreaks of the plague in London.

Today the castle has been greatly revamped as a tourist attraction and boasts an aviary, a maze (laid in 1988), a grotto and a golf course. It also claims to house the only museum of dog collars anywhere in the world.

The castle, as it stands today, boast several towers: the Constable's Tower, The Maiden's Tower and the Water Tower. One more, termed the Gloriette, is of special significance. It is on the smallest of the islands and was built by Edward I in 1278 for his wife, Queen Eleanor (and is thus alternatively known as the Queen's Tower).

Such a beautiful setting, of course, could never escape the attention of film makers and TV producers and so the castle has featured in several films and dramas etc. It was the setting for the aristocratic family seat of the d'Ascoynes in the 1949 film *Kind Hearts and Coronets*, starring Alec Guinness; the *Doctor Who* episode 'The Androids of Tara' was shot there in 1978 and more recently the *Antiques Roadshow*, presented by Fiona Bruce, came from the castle's croquet lawn in July 2008.

## HEVER CASTLE

Not very far away from Leeds Castle and also nestling in the Weald of Kent is another castle with a history full of romance and tragedy. Hever Castle, forever associated in most people's minds with Henry VIII and Anne Boleyn, is yet another example of Henry's eye for a beautiful building. The moated structure, like Leeds Castle, is set in beautiful countryside and surrounded by enchanting gardens guaranteed to gladden the heart (and eye!) of professional and amateur gardeners alike. There are some who claim that Hever's gardens outshine even those of Leeds Castle and that they are the most beautiful gardens in England. And they might be right.

It is difficult, if not downright impossible, for a visitor, observing and no doubt admiring the impressive building in its charming setting, to imagine that the whole thing started life as nothing more than a lowly farmhouse. If history is to be believed, William I made a gift of the land and old Saxon farmstead to a Norman nobleman Walter de Hevere (or d'evere) who decided that he would strip the old building and develop it into a manor house. Then, in about 1270, his descendent William de Hevere invested time and money into converting it into a castle, complete with moat. Almost two hundred years later, in 1459 to be exact, the castle was acquired by a certain Sir Geoffrey Bullen, originally a Norfolk silk merchant but now Mayor of London. The estate remained in the Bullen family and in the sixteenth century it was inherited by Thomas who had a daughter named Anne. And she of course, after a certain distortion of the surname, came down through history to us as Anne Boleyn, the second wife of Henry VIII.

Visitors to Hever Castle come face to face with many object and artefacts connecting them with the castle's history and in particular with the time Anne Boleyn spent there. Amazement is the usual response to the tiny size of the bedroom where she slept as a child, an emotional response matched only by feelings of fascination for the intricate locks on the doors which Henry himself had fixed to the room where he slept on his frequent visits. But perhaps the most disturbing artefact is Anne's own prayer book, or Book of Hours, which is still there for all to see. It contains the lines, written in Anne's own hand:

'Remember me when you do pray,
that hope doth lead from day to day.'

This couplet, of no particular poetic or artistic merit, is invested with a certain poignancy when we remember that this little book is reputedly all she took with her as she mounted the scaffold for her rendezvous with the executioner.

When Sir Thomas Boleyn died in 1539 (some say of a broken heart) Henry requisitioned the castle and then later gave it as part of his divorce settlement to Anne of Cleves (or, more correctly, Anna von Jülich-Kleve-Berg) in 1540. She lived there until her death in 1557.

## ROCHESTER CASTLE

Unlike most castles in Kent, which tend to stand outside the towns they are associated with, Rochester Castle stands in the centre of Rochester itself, towering over its houses, shops and schools like a giant sentinel. But it was not always such an imposing edifice; in fact, its origins are as humble as those of Hever, although they stretch back much further in time. Like its counterpart at Dover, Rochester Castle began life as a Roman settlement, and archaeological evidence suggests that there was some kind of defensive structure on the site even before that.

The castle as it stands today is yet another prime example of Norman architecture and was built between the years 1087 and 1089 by Gundulf, who was then Bishop of Rochester. Its keep, towering 113ft above Rochester's Castle Hill, is among the tallest of such towers in the whole of England. Its walls are a daunting 13ft thick (at their maximum) which must have made the whole fortress appear virtually impenetrable to an attacking army before the advent of powerful artillery. This explains why, during the first years of its history, the castle was subjected to three prolonged sieges: storming the walls was just not an option.

The first siege came about not long after the Norman Conquest. The city and castle had been gifted by William to his half-brother Odo, Bishop of Bayeux, who, before his fall from grace in the king's eyes and subsequent imprisonment in 1082, had exerted great power throughout the whole land and not just in Kent where he had been appointed earl.

William died in 1087 and Odo was set free in 1088 just in time to get involved in the dissent being voiced by some of the Norman barons who were dissatisfied with William's son, Rufus, the new king. Odo supported the rebels and so found himself on the losing side after Rufus besieged the castle and forced the defenders into a humiliating surrender. The king, however, seems to have taken a lenient view of his rebellious subjects' actions and allowed them to march out of the castle unmolested. But they were obliged to surrender their lands and property and Odo, who must have decided that it was time to opt for the quiet life, left England, never to return, and settled once again in Normandy.

The next king who had to deal with rebellious barons was John (r. 1166–99). He also found out just how sturdy the walls were and, just like Rufus, was forced to give up all thoughts of a full-frontal attack. He brought up his ballistas and mangonels, which hurled huge boulders at the mighty walls, but they hardly dented them and so he was forced to use another tactic, namely the siege. This lasted over two months but was showing no signs of achieving the desired outcome and so John had no option but to attempt the extremely dangerous technique of undermining the walls. He ordered his men to undermine the tower on the south-eastern side of the battlements by digging deep tunnels under the walls. They slaved away for days mining out the earth under the constant threat of being killed outright or buried alive beneath thousands of tons of earth and falling masonry. But eventually the task was completed and the tower walls came crashing down. John had his entrée and was able to take the castle and arrest the rebels.

The next time the castle was subjected to a siege was during the civil war occasioned by yet another rebellion in 1264, when Simon de Montfort had something of a disagreement with Henry III. This time it was the king's men who held the castle and the rebels who attempted to seize control. Led by de Montfort they attacked and, if contemporary accounts are to be believed, went on something of a rampage of wanton blood-letting. Many loyal subjects were killed and eventually the defenders of the castle were forced to withdraw into the keep. It was at this moment that Simon de Montfort decided on a siege but, after a relatively short time, his patience got the better of him and he opted for taking a leaf out of John's book and decided to undermine the walls of the keep. This time, however, the tactic failed or at least was not given time to succeed. Before the undermining was complete de Montfort received intelligence that the king was approaching with an army of well-armed soldiers and immediately conceded that, on this occasion at least, discretion would be the better part of valour. Rochester Castle was never besieged again.

What followed was a period of decline and neglect. The age of the majestic castles was over and most became little more than extremely expensive white elephants. By the seventeenth century Rochester Castle was in a sorry state and was slowly but surely deteriorating. By the mid-nineteenth century something had to be done. Fortunately the obvious answer, demolition, was not the one chosen and the grounds were taken over by the City of Rochester and turned into a municipal park. In 1965 the responsibility for upkeep of the castle was assumed by the Ministry of Public Buildings and Works and some years later, in 1984, it was taken under the wing of English Heritage where it has remained ever since.

## THE CASTLES OF THE DOWNS

Henry VIII was a worried man. After his shabby treatment of Catherine of Aragón England became something of a pariah among European nations. Henry had offended much of Catholic Europe and when France and Spain signed a treaty in 1538 he probably suspected some sort of Catholic alliance against him was taking shape. An invasion by a combined force of two of the most powerful nations in Europe must have seemed at least enough of a distinct possibility (if not an absolute certainty) to keep him awake at night. And his solution to the nightmare was to build more castles.

All in all Henry set about building thirty new castles in those parts of the country which had reasonably good landing grounds for invading troops. In Kent the main 'Device Forts', as they were known, were the 'Castles of the Downs', specifically Deal Castle, Walmer Castle, Sandgate Castle (1539–40) and Sandown Castle built in the same year (which should not be confused with a castle of the same name on the Isle of Wight). Generally speaking the design of these sixteenth-century defensive constructions differed considerable from their Norman cousins as they had to take into account the changes in warfare and battlefield technology. Artillery now played a much greater role and the castle defenders could inflict serious damage on an enemy at a far greater, and largely anonymous, distance. The military tacticians of the day also realised that curved walls could deflect incoming cannonballs more efficiently than angular, straight battlements which would stop a cannonball mid-flight but at the same time suffer considerable damage in the process. Also, obviously, a low profile would present an enemy with a much smaller target and be far more difficult to hit. Walmer (1539) and Deal (1539) Castles (Sandown has long-since disappeared) are consequently squat and circular, and encapsulate perfectly much of the new developments in the philosophy and technology of combat. However, many of the old fortress features survived so visitors to Walmer and Deal castles today can still see the portcullis, the murderholes and drawbridges which were such a prominent part of their Norman ancestors.

# CASTLE ARCHITECTURE

## Curtain Wall
This is simply the technical term for the wall surrounding and encompassing all the buildings and land on which the castle stands. It was usually made of solid rock and could be up to 13ft thick.

## Barbican
A massive and heavily protected gate-house. It also housed all the mechanism for operating the drawbridge and portcullis.

## Portcullis
A very heavy gate-like structure which descended vertically from the barbican and acted as a protective barrier to anyone attempting to rush the drawbridge before it could be raised.

## Murder hole
An opening in the floor of the barbican directly above the portcullis through which boiling oil could be poured, boulders could be hurled and arrows could be loosed at attackers beneath.

## Keep
A tower within the castle grounds to which the defenders would retreat as a last resort if they were being beaten by the opposing forces. The staircase in such towers curved upwards in a clockwise direction. This meant that attackers, trying to fight their way upstairs, found it difficult to wield their swords, especially if they were right-handed.

## Motte
The mound which forms the site on which the castle is built. This was a feature particularly of Norman castles.

## Bailey
The open ground at the centre of the castle, similar to a courtyard. The word is derived from the Norman French *baille*, meaning enclosure. The central criminal court in London, known as The Old Bailey, is derived from the same word as it stands on what

used to be the 'bailey' within the city walls. Also, the oldest part of Folkestone is still known as 'The Bayle' which suggests that at one time there was a fortress or castle on the site.

## Oubliette

A bottle-shaped hole in the ground which could be accessed only through a trap door. A prisoner would be lowered through the trap door, as would his food and drink. The origin of the word is the French verb *oublier*, 'to forget', as presumably, once in there a prisoner could easily be forgotten.

## Donjon

This was the original name for a keep in a Norman castle. As time went by, however, and the tower was used mainly as a holding place for prisoners, it was realised that there would be far less opportunity for escape or rescue if the 'donjons' were constructed underground. This became the normal practice and the word itself evolved into what we now know as 'dungeons'.

## Buttery

Every castle needed one, but it had nothing to do with dairy products. The word is derived from Norman French *botte* meaning 'cask' and so the 'buttery' was where the casks or barrels of wine and beer were stored. And the man responsible for their safe keeping was the 'butler'.

## Solar

This was the Great Chamber which would have been occupied by the lords and ladies and their immediate entourage. The root of the word is the Latin *sol*, meaning 'sun', as these rooms were usually situated on the upper floors and were the brightest and sunniest.

## Machicolations

A variation on the murder holes, machicolations were usually found running along the battlements and would have been manned by soldiers hurling stones, etc. down on the attackers beneath the walls. The word is derived from the Norman French *machicoler*, meaning 'to crush'.

### Garderobe

This is the old French word that has given us the modern English 'wardrobe' and was a place in a castle where robes and other articles of value were kept. But it also doubled as the castle toilets and the waste matter was disposed of via primitive plumbing straight into the moat. It has been suggested that the cloaks and other items of clothing were stored in the loo because it was believed that the stench killed moths!

### Batter

This was basically an addition to the base of the outer walls comprising hardened material angled at 45 degrees so that rocks dropped from above would bounce off and kill or injure attacking soldiers.

### Talus

A sloping, as opposed to a perpendicular, protective outer wall. The slope served two main purposes: it prevented siege engines from getting closer to the wall than the base and it also meant that there was nowhere for the attackers to hide from the defenders' field of vision.

### Adulterine

Not an architectural term in itself but it applied to any castle which was built without the permission of the reigning monarch if such permission should have been granted before construction began.

# 4

# LITERARY KENT

From the very earliest days of English literature writers have flourished in Kent. Many had little choice in the matter and were born in the county simply because their mothers happened to have the good fortune to be there when their 'items of mortality' (a Dickens phrase) chose to make an entrance into this world. Others, for one reason or another, settled in Kent on a temporary or permanent basis, and made it the base for their creative activity.

## WRITERS BORN IN KENT

**John Lyly (c. 1553/4–1606).** Born somewhere in Kent (the exact spot is unknown) he is known to have been brought up in Canterbury where he was educated at King's School at about the same time as Christopher Marlowe. We do know that he took his MA at Magdalene College, Oxford, in 1575 but he was an indifferent student. He left university with a reputation for his keen wit rather than his academic excellence and decided to devote himself to his writing soon after leaving university. In 1578 and 1580 respectively Lyly wrote the two works for which he is most renowned: *Eupheus or An Anatomy of Wit* and *Eupheus and his England*. His 'euphuistic' style, as it came to be known, was extremely ornate, flowery and peppered with moral maxims. His plays include *Campaspe* (c. 1584); *Gallathea* (1584); *Endymion: The Man in the Moon* (1586–7); *Love's Metamorphosis* (1589) and *Midas* (1589).

Lyly's most famous quotes include:

'Night hath a thousand eyes' – *Maides Metamorphose*
'Children and fools speak true' – *Endymion*
'There can be no great smoke arise but there must be some fire'
    – *Euphues*
'All's fair in love and war' – *attributed*

**Sir Philip Sidney (1554–86)**. Linguist, scholar, diplomat and
a passionately patriotic gentleman, Philip Sidney was born in
Penshurst, the eldest son of Sir Henry Sidney (who had been a
friend and confidant of Edward II) and Lady Mary Dudley.
From 1564 to 1568 he was a scholar at Shrewsbury School
under the tutelage of one of the leading educators of the time,
Thomas Ashton. In 1586 he went up to Christ Church, Oxford,
where he concentrated on the study of languages. He was then
posted to Paris in 1572 where he was employed in the embassy
under the then ambassador, Sir Francis Walsingham. No doubt
he enjoyed the pleasurable round of ambassadorial duties and
elegant soirées, but he also became involved in the frightening
events of the St Bartholomew's Day Massacre when thousands
of Protestants were slaughtered by angry Catholics. Soon
afterwards he embarked on further travels throughout Europe,
visiting Vienna, Prague and even getting as far as Poland. From
1575 he spent more time at home in England where he became
a courtier and then, in 1578, he turned his hand to writing and
produced his first work *The Lady of May*. This was followed by
*Arcadia, A Defence of Poesy* in 1580. Also in 1580 he began
*Astrophil and Stella* which circulated at first in manuscript form
and was not published until five years after the poet's death. In
the 1580s Sidney was appointed Master of Ordnance and was
tasked with overseeing the nation's preparations for the war with
Spain that was looming on the horizon. Half-way through the
decade he was appointed Governor of Flushing (Vlissingen) in
Holland and in September of the following year he was involved
in a shoot-out with Spanish troops. A musket ball hit him in the
thigh and, although the wound was serious, he was able to make
a reasonable recovery. But then the wound turned gangrenous
and he died on 17 October 1586. His body was returned to
England where he was given an elaborate funeral with pomp and
ceremony almost equal to that seen at the funerals of royalty.

Sidney's most famous quotes include:

'Thank God for tea. What would the world be without tea?'
– *Lady Holland's Memoir*. NB: Although tea was virtually
unknown in England at this time, Sidney would probably
have come across it in Venice where it was already a
popular beverage.
'The trouble with cats is that they've got no tact.'
'Eagles we see fly alone and they are but sheep which always
herd together.'

**Aphra Behn (1640–89).** Details about this lady are somewhat
hazy. It has been claimed that she was born in Wye, near Ashford,
but this is still a moot point. We do know, however, that she was
christened Aphra Johnson, the daughter of Bartholomew and
Elizabeth Derham, on 14 December 1640 at Harbledown church,
near Canterbury. She grew up to be the first professional woman
writer in English literature and, as a Restoration dramatist, was
second only to John Dryden in prolificacy. She wrote eighteen
plays including *The Forced Marriage* (1670), *The Amorous Prince*
(1671), *The Rover* (1677), *The Second Part of the Rover* (1681),
*The Lucky Chance* (1686), *The Lucky Mistake* (1689) and *The
Roundheads* (1681). She also wrote prose works and in 1688
produced *The Fair Jilt, Agnes de Castro* and the work for which
she is most famous, *Oroonoko*.

For some reason, which has never been fully explained, she
went off to live in Surinam from 1663 to 1664, where she met
and married a Dutch trader, Mr Behn. She is also know to have
become involved in the murky world of espionage, spying for
Charles II, but she gave this up and decided to make her way
in life as a full-time writer. Considering her relative present-day
obscurity it is somewhat surprising that, when she died in 1689,
she was buried in Poets' Corner in Westminster Abbey. This is an
achievement for any writer, but an astounding feat for a woman
writer in the seventeenth century.

Aphra Behn came out with some clever quotes in her time:

'Faith, Sir, we are here today and gone tomorrow.' –
*The Lucky Mistake*

'A brave world, Sir, full of religion, knavery and change: we
shall shortly see better days.' – *The Roundheads*
'Come away: poverty is catching.' – *The Second Part of the
Rover*
'There is no sinner like a young saint.' – *The Rover*

**Christopher Marlowe (1564–93).** The son of a wealthy
Canterbury cobbler, Marlowe was born in the same year as
Shakespeare and is believed to have had a hand in showing the
Bard how to write. Marlowe was educated at King's School and
then went up to Cambridge (Corpus Christi), and graduated
in 1584. His many absences from his studies and displays of
conspicuous wealth during his attendances have led many to
suspect that he was a government spy and was frequently sent
away on undercover missions for which he was handsomely paid.
He held very unorthodox views and was, in fact, an atheist at a
time when atheism was considered blasphemous and punishable
by death. By 1587 Marlowe was living in London where he had
embarked on a career as a playwright. He was stabbed to death
in what seems to have been a brawl outside a pub in Deptford
in 1593. His main works include *Tamburlaine the Great* (part
one: 1587; part two: *c.* 1587), *Doctor Faustus* (1588); *The Jew
of Malta* (1589) and *Edward the Second* (printed 1592). Some
critics maintain that the play *The Taming of the Shrew*, normally
attributed to Shakespeare, was in fact written by Marlowe.
Among Marlowe's most famous quotes are:

'Comparisons are odious' – the poem 'Hero and Leander'
'Was this the face that launched a thousand ships?' – *Dr
Faustus*
'Stand still, you ever-moving spheres of heaven, / That time
may cease and midnight never come.' – *Dr Faustus*

**William Hazlitt (1778–1830).** Born in Maidstone, the son of a
Unitarian minister, young William was an extremely clever boy who
demonstrated an intellectual grasp of history and current affairs
well beyond his years. The family went to live in Ireland and then
America for a while and on their return settled in Shropshire. From
very early in his life, William was expected to enter the church but,

*Remains of the church in Canterbury where Christopher Marlowe was christened. The clock, street lamp and bollards are obviously later additions.*

something of a loner and very much his own man, he set his heart
on being a painter. Then in 1804 or 1805 he had another change
of mind and decided on a life devoted to literature and philosophy.
His political views at this time were not guaranteed to make him
the most popular thinker in the country. He was passionately
concerned about the condition of the poor and his radical thoughts
were planted in firm Republican convictions. But at the same time
he was an admirer of Napoleon and a staunch supporter of the
French Revolution. As a journalist, critic, grammarian and essayist,
Hazlitt's contribution to English letters lies mainly in his essays
and political writings, which include *The Spirit of the Age* (1825),
*The English Comic Writers* (1819), *An Essay on the Principles of
Human Action* (1805), *Characters of Shakespeare's Plays* (1817),
*Political Essays with Sketches of Public Characters* (1819) and
*Notes of a Journey through France and Italy* (1826).

Hazlitt's quotes include:

'Man is a make-believe animal: he is never so truly himself
  as when he is acting the part.'
'I would spend my whole life travelling if I could
  somewhere borrow another life to spend at home.'
'If you give an audience a chance it will do half your acting
  for you.'
'It is not fit that every man should travel; it makes a wise
  man better and a fool worse.'

**H.G. Wells (1866–1946).** Herbert George Wells was born in
Bromley on 21 September 1866 and grew up to be one of England's
foremost men of letters. He was an essayist, historian, futurist
and very much a political animal. He is generally recognised as
one of the initiators of the genre we now know as science fiction.
His background was anything but privileged: his mother was a
maid and his father a shopkeeper. Family circumstances meant
that young Herbert had to leave school at fourteen and take up
an apprenticeship in a draper's store and the experience he gained
there gave him the material for his first forays into the world of
literature: *The Wheels of Chance* (1896) and *Kipps* (1905). In
1884 he won a scholarship to the Royal College of Science, where
he studied until 1887 then, in 1890, he gained a BSc in Zoology

*Spade House in Folkestone where H.G. Wells lived between 1901 and 1909. This is where he wrote* Kipps, Tono-Bungay *and* Ann Veronica.

as an external student at London University. On the world's stage he was an outspoken critic of class divisions, was a member of the Fabian Society and for a while was seduced by events in the early days of the Soviet Union. He was taken in by Stalin whom he described as a fair and honest man. Wells's literary output was enormous and his most famous works include: *The Invisible Man* (1897), *War of the Worlds* (1898), *The History of Mr Polly* (1910), *The Time Machine* (1895), *The Island of Doctor Moreau* (1896), *The Shape of Things to Come* (1933), *A Short History of the World* (1922) and *The Outline of History* (1920).

**Russell Thorndike (1885–1972).** Born in Rochester, his sister was the actress Sybil Thorndike. Like his sister, Russell seemed destined for a life of acting and did enjoy a life on stage and screen for over forty years. But he was never as famous as Sybil because he was always pulled in the direction of writing as well. His first attempts at the series that was to bring him literary acclaim, the *Dr Syn* novels (all about eighteenth-century smugglers in the Dymchurch area of Kent) appeared in 1915 just about the same time as he joined the army, together with his brother Frank. Frank was killed and Russell took part in the disastrous Gallipoli campaign where he was so badly wounded that he was discharged from the army and repatriated to England. Once recovered, he resumed his acting career but continued with his real passion, writing, and enjoyed parallel occupations right up to his death in 1972. His writings include novels and plays such as the Dr Syn novels, *The House of Jeffreys* (1943), *Children of the Garter* (1937), *Saul* (1906), *The Tragedy of Mr Punch* (1924), *The Shadow of Doctor Syn* (1944) and *The Scarecrow Rides* (1935).

**Siegfried Sassoon (1886–1967).** Known mainly as one of the War Poets (together with Wilfred Owen, et al), Siegfried Loraine Sassoon was born into an Anglo-Jewish family in 1886 in Matfield, near Tunbridge Wells. Despite his German-sounding first name there are no German connections at all in his family history; his first name (which must have caused him some embarrassment at times) was nothing more than the result of his mother's passion for Wagnerian operas. He was educated at The New Beacon Preparatory School in Sevenoaks, then Marlborough College before he went up to Clare College, Cambridge, to read History and Law. But he did not stay the course and left without a degree; instead of studying he preferred to spend his time hunting and playing cricket.

When war broke out he was among the first to enlist and was a courageous, highly decorated soldier. But he became disillusioned with war when he witnessed the disparity between the jingoistic patriotism fed constantly to those at home and the horrors of the battlefield. His poems countered much of the official morale-boosting propaganda in the press with descriptions of the carnage, the blood-soaked trenches, the fear, the psychological torment and the excruciating nightmares experienced by the terrified 'heroes' who were forced, often at bayonet-point, to go 'over the top'. His first attempt at writing was *The Daffodil Murder* (a parody of a poem by John Masefield) which he wrote in 1913. This was followed by a constant stream of works, poetry and prose, including: *The Old Huntsman* (1917), *Blighters* (1918), *Counter*

*Attack* (1918), *Dreamers* (1918), *Everyone Sang* (1918), *Suicide in the Trenches* (1918), *Memoirs of a Fox-Hunting Man* (1928), *Memoirs of an Infantry Officer* (1930) and *Sherston's Progress* (1936).

**Vita Sackville-West (1892–1962).** Born in 1892 at Knole House, Sevenoaks, Victoria Mary Sackville-West was a prolific authoress (prose and poetry) and renowned gardener. She never came to terms with the fact that, on the death of her father, the laws of primogeniture which were still the law of the land in the 1940s prevented Victoria from inheriting the family home and her uncle became the legal owner.

Her personal life was highly unconventional, especially for those times. She married the diplomat Harold Nicholson but they were quite open to each other about their promiscuous homosexual affairs. Vita had many lovers, the most notable of whom was Virginia Woolf, who wrote about the affair in her own novel *Orlando*. Vita's first published work was a long poem entitled 'The Land' which won her the Hawthornden Prize in 1927. She was only the second poet to win this prize twice as it was awarded to her again in 1927 for her *Collected Poems*. She went on to write many more works including: *The Edwardians* (1930), *All Passion Spent* (1931), *Grand Canyon* (1942), *Heritage* (1919) and *No Signposts in the Sea* (1961). In addition, she translated *Elegies from the Castle of Duino* by the German writer Rainer Maria Rilke and wrote biographies of Joan of Arc, St Teresa of Avila and Thérèse of Lisieux (the latter two in the volume entitled *The Eagle and the Dove*) and of Aphra Behn. Apart from her writing she was a passionate gardener and she and her husband bought Sissinghurst Castle in a run-down, dilapidated state and transformed the grounds into the magnificent gardens which survive today as the property of the National Trust.

**Frederick Forsyth (1938–).** Born in Ashford, the son of a furrier, Frederick Forsyth was educated at Tonbridge School and then went off to study at the University of Granada in Spain. When the time came for him to do his National Service (1956–8) he joined the Royal Air Force and, at the tender age of nineteen, qualified as a pilot, making him one of the youngest pilots ever in the RAF's history. Back in Civvy Street he became a journalist, working for Reuters and the BBC. He was sent to report on the Nigerian Civil War (the Nigerian state against the breakaway region of Biafra) in 1969, but fell foul of his bosses. Too many of his reports appeared to show bias towards the Biafrans and so he was 'relieved of his post'. On his return to England he wrote his first book *The Biafra Story* (1969) which was followed shortly afterwards by the publication of his first full-length novel *The Day of the Jackal* (1971). This was an immediate success which brought international fame and won him the Edgar Allan Poe Award for Best Novel. By now he was firmly on track to carve out a career for himself as a full-time writer and the novels came thick and fast: between 1971 and 2006 he wrote something in the order of sixteen novels including *The Odessa File, The Fourth Protocol, The Dogs of War, Avenger* and, most recently *The Afghan* and *The Cobra* . His style is rapid, journalistic and action-packed and his themes involve international relations, wars, assassinations (actual or attempted) and the workings of the secret services. Politically, Frederick Forsyth is staunchly Royalist, Conservative and deeply Euro-sceptic. His appearances on TV have frequently involved political discussions in which he expresses himself in a forthright manner.

## WRITERS BORN OUTSIDE KENT

**Geoffrey Chaucer (*c*. 1343–1400).** Widely recognised as 'the father of English literature', Chaucer was born in London but is inextricably associated with Kent because of his major work *The Canterbury Tales,* a collection of stories based on the various characters who undertook the Spring pilgrimage from London to Canterbury. Breaking with the established tradition, Chaucer told the tales in ordinary, vernacular Middle English, rather than

Latin or French. There are considerable gaps in our knowledge of his life, but we do know that his father had been a vintner, that Geoffrey had been pageboy to the Countess of Ulster and that, at one stage in his life, he was a soldier. Documents of the time suggest that King Edward III paid the grand sum of £16 as a contribution to his ransom when he was captured by the French during the Hundred Years War. Somewhat paradoxically, writing for the man who made such a lasting impact on English literature was not a full-time occupation. He earned his money as a civil servant ('comptroller' was his actual title) in the Customs House based in Aldgate, London. The circles he moved in were the highest in the land; in 1367 (when he was about twenty-seven) he became a *valet de chambre* at court and travelled widely in Europe on the king's business. The king must have taken a liking to the young poet as at one point he bestowed upon him a pension of 'a gallon of wine per day' for life, although we cannot be sure of the nature of the service that warranted such an award. In about 1375 Chaucer was appointed a Commissioner for Peace in Kent and became the Member of Parliament for the county as well. The manner of his death in 1400 is unclear. He may have died a natural death but there are those who opine that he was murdered, although it is not clear why or by whom. All that can be said with any certainty is that he was buried in Poets' Corner in Westminster Abbey, the first recipient of the honour. In addition to *The Canterbury Tales*, Chaucer's works include *The Book of the Duchess* (1369/1374); *The House of Fame, Parlement of Foules (Parliament of Fowls), The Legend of the Good Woman* and *Troilus and Criseyde*. Chaucer was also fascinated by philosophy, medieval science, astrology and astronomy (which, in those days, were more or less the same thing) and wrote a non-fiction work called *Treatise on the Astrolabe*.

Among Chaucer's quotes are:

'Murder will out.' – *Canterbury Tales, The Nonne Priest's Tale*

'He was a very parfit gentil knight.' – *Canterbury Tales, The Knight's Tale*

'He knew the taverns wel in every toun.' – *Canterbury Tales, The Friar's Tale*

**Charles Dickens (1812–70).** Not even the most cursory glance at the history of English literature would be complete without mention of Charles John Huffam Dickens who, few would doubt, is the greatest novelist England has ever seen. His enormously prolific output of novels and short stories has kept generations of readers occupied for many hours of rapt enjoyment as they encounter such unforgettable characters as Oliver Twist, Philip Pirrip (aka Pip), Miss Havisham, Sam Weller, Tiny Tim and countless others among the 989 personas he created and brought to life during his writing career. Charles Dickens was born in Portsmouth in 1812 but the family soon moved to Chatham in Kent where his father was a navy clerk. He received some basic education as a child but the family fell upon hard times and his father ended up in Marshalsea debtors' prison, which readers soon encounter in *Little Dorrit*. Forced to help out with the family finances, young Charles, still only a boy, had to work ten hours a day in a factory near today's Charing Cross station pasting labels on tins of shoe polish. When, as an adult, he began writing novels, he was able to draw on the dreadful conditions he experienced at first-hand as a victim of child labour. He also crammed his works with damning descriptions of the depravity and cruelty engendered by the crippling, destructive poverty he saw all around him. Victorian England, for the vast majority of the populace, was not a pleasant place in which to live or grow up, and Dickens pulled no punches in his descriptions of what he saw as the unjustifiably degrading existence of all but the privileged few. Many of his stories are set in Kent, a county he came to know and love and where he spent most of his adult life. At various times he lived in Folkestone, Canterbury, Rochester, Broadstairs and, as soon as the royalties from his writings allowed it, bought Gads Hill Place in Higham near Rochester. It was here that, on 9 June 1870 he had a stroke and died. He left instructions that he wanted a quiet burial, but his wishes were ignored and he is buried along with many of his illustrious fellow-writers in Poets' Corner, Westminster Abbey. The works for which he will long be remembered, loved and admired include *The Pickwick Papers* (1837), *The Old Curiosity Shop* (1841), *Oliver Twist* (1839), *Nicholas Nickleby* (1839), *A Christmas Carol* (1843),

*David Copperfield* (1850), *A Tale of Two Cities* (1859), *Bleak House* (1853) and *Great Expectations* (1861).

Dickens quotes include:

'The law is a ass – a idiot.' – *Oliver Twist*

Kent, sir – everybody knows Kent – apples, cherries, hops
and women.' – *Pickwick Papers*

'The melancholy truth is that even great men have their
poor relations.' – *Bleak House*

'Poverty and oysters always seem to go together.' –
*Pickwick Papers*

**Joseph Conrad (1857–1924).** Joseph Conrad achieved what has
to be one of the greatest feats in the history of world literature. He
became one of the foremost writers of a country whose language,
English, he did not learn until he was in his twenties. He was born
into a cultured Polish family living in what is now Ukraine but at
the time was part of the Russian Empire. He grew up speaking
Polish, his father taught him French and no doubt he also spoke
Ukrainian and Russian. He was born in Berdychev in 1857 where
he was christened Jósef Teodor Konrad Korzeniowski. His father
was a translator but was also fiercely anti-Russian and was exiled
by the authorities for revolutionary activity to a remote part of
Russia's frozen north. By the age of eleven Jósef was orphaned and
taken into the house of an uncle. In his teens, in order to escape
military service in the Russian Army he left home and made his
way to Marseilles where he embarked (literally and figuratively) on
a life at sea. He travelled the world, much of the time as a carefree
adventurer, did a spot of gun-running, was stricken with malaria,
attempted suicide, and saw the darker side of human behaviour.
He was sickened by the hypocritical rhetoric of the European
colonialists who claimed to be bringing Christianity to places
such as Africa when all they were doing in fact was plundering the
continent of its riches. Allied to his naturally depressive nature,
his experiences gave him a grimly pessimistic view of life (which
he saw as pointless and leading to nothing but eternal darkness
and silence) and human nature. But his adventures and ideas
which they engendered became the stuff of which his novels
are made. When he gave up the life of a wanderer and sailor he

eventually settled in Kent, living first, from 1898 to 1907, in a farm house (Pent Farm, a few miles north of Folkestone) which he rented from a fellow writer, Ford Madox Ford, and then moved to Bishopsbourne just outside Canterbury where he lived with his wife and children until his death from a heart attack in 1924. He is buried in Canterbury and his gravestone bears his original Polish surname. During his career he wrote many short stories and novels, the main ones including *Almayer's Folly* (1895), *An Outcast of the Islands* (1896), *The Nigger of the Narcissus* (1897), *Typhoon* (1902), *Nostromo* (1904), *Under Western Eyes* (1911). His major novels *Lord Jim* (1900) and *Heart of Darkness* (1899) were written while he was staying at Pent Farm.

Conrad's quotes include:

'You shall judge of a man by his foes as well as by his friends.' – *Lord Jim*

'The belief in a supernatural source of evil is not necessary; men alone are quite capable of every wickedness.' – *Under Western Eyes*

'The sea never changes and its works, for all the talk of men, are wrapped in mystery.' – *Typhoon*

**H.E. Bates (1905–74).** Known to most people now through the TV adaptation of his *The Darling Buds of May*, Herbert Ernest Bates was born in Northamptonshire and only moved down to Kent after he had married his childhood sweetheart, Madge Cox. They began their married life in the village of Little Chart, just outside Ashford, and stayed there for the rest of their days, transforming the overgrown wilderness surrounding the house (actually it was a derelict granary) into a wonderful garden. Herbert and Madge derived enormous pleasure from gardening and in fact he, a man of the soil through and through, wrote gardening books before he turned his hand to fiction. And even when his short stories began to appear they were redolent with descriptions of the old country ways and farming before the advent of chemicals, weed-killers and heavy machinery. All his works remind the reader of what country life was like before the transformation of what had been agricultural practice for hundreds of years. When war broke out he joined the RAF where he was tasked (and this must have been a godsend for a writer) with writing stories about brave airmen and their daring exploits over enemy territory for consumption back home. The stories flowed from the tip of his pen and readers on the home front were entertained by derring-do adventure stories written by a certain Flying Officer X, the pseudonym under which Bates preferred to write. After the war Bates maintained his prodigious output producing a novel every year, in addition to short stories, several of which were adapted for film or television (or both). His best known works include *Charlotte's Row* (1931), *The Woman who had Imagination* (1934), *Love for Lydia* (1952), *My Uncle Silas* (1939), *Fair Stood the Wind for France* (1944) and *The Jacaranda Tree* (1949). His novel set in the Kent village of Pluckley (just a few miles from Little Chart), *The Darling Buds of May,* was the inspiration behind the Hollywood film of 1959, *The Mating Game.* His *Purple Plain* (1947) was adapted for a film starring Gregory Peck and was so successful that it provided him with financial security for the rest of his life. He was awarded a CBE in 1973, but perhaps the highest critical accolade was paid by Graham Greene who said that H.E. Bates was Britain's successor to Chekhov. He died in 1974 and is buried in Canterbury.

**Ian Lancaster Fleming (1908–64).** Fleming is probably the most successful author of the twentieth century associated with Kent. Tall, sophisticated, elegant and debonair he was the archetypal James Bond, the fictitious central character of the fourteen spy novels which he published in the 1950s and '60s. He was born in Mayfair, London, and spent his holidays on the family estate in Oxfordshire. His father, Valentine Fleming, was a Tory MP who believed in a no-nonsense upbringing for his children. He sent Ian and his brother Peter to the Durford School in Dorset, an austere, almost Draconian institution where the headmaster was a fervent believer in the value of early-morning cold baths, strict discipline and hours of Latin. After Durford, Ian became a pupil at Eton, but was unhappy there and did not really fit in, although he did excel at games and seems to have acquired an interest in languages there which stood him in good stead for the rest of his life. During the 1930s he spent some time in Kitzbühel, Austria, and then Munich University where he was able to acquire a more than just adequate fluency in German. Following this his mother sent him to Geneva where he was able to add a good grasp of French to his repertoire of languages. Strangely, his linguistic gifts were not enough to secure him acceptance into the Foreign Office, the career path he had set himself, but he was offered a position with Reuters news agency. This gave him a chance to travel and visit some pretty exotic places, including Moscow, and then, at the outbreak of war, he was recruited into Naval Intelligence and immediately found himself in the shadowy world of espionage. His experiences and the contacts he made during this part of his life gave him a rich fund of material on which he was able to draw when he turned his hand to writing. When he did so, the novels and short stories just flowed off the tip of his pen: *Casino Royale* (1953), *Live and Let Die* (1954), *Moonraker* (1955), *Diamonds are Forever* (1956), *From Russia with Love* (1957), *Dr No* (1958), *Goldfinger* (1959), *Thunderball* (1961), *The Spy who Loved Me* (1962), *On Her Majesty's Secret Service* (1963), *You Only Live Twice* (1964) and *The Man with the Golden Gun,* published in 1965, a year

*Ian Fleming's temporary home at St Margaret's Bay.*

after Fleming's death. What many people do not realise is that Ian Fleming also wrote the children's story *Chitty Chitty Bang Bang*, which was published in 1964.

During the mid-1950s Ian Fleming bought a house right down at the water's edge in St Margaret's Bay, near Dover, and then lived in Bekesbourne, just outside Canterbury. A keen sportsman, he liked to spend as much time as possible at the Royal St George's golf club in Sandwich and it was during a visit there in 1964 that he suffered a heart attack. He was rushed to hospital in Canterbury but died at 1 o'clock the following morning, 12 August. Cruelly, it was his only son Caspar's twefth birthday.

**T.S. Eliot (1888–1965).** Thomas Stearnes Eliot was born in America (St Louis, Missouri, to be precise) and enrolled as a student at the Smith Academy in 1898 where his studies followed a decidedly classical path. He studied French, German, Latin and Greek (he added Sanskrit to his linguistic achievements later in life) and then Philosophy at Harvard. Such an academic background is of prime importance when we try to understand (or even just read) much of his poetry. Most of it is so crammed with classical quotations and allusions that all but the most erudite scholars can make head or tail of his works only by constant reference to clear and comprehensive crib notes. His work is highly cerebral and while making constant references to the literature of the past is clearly an attempt to create a literature for the future.

Eliot left America in 1914 and, after a brief stay in Germany and France, took up residence in England and later, in 1927, took British nationality. He studied at Oxford University and then moved to London where he had a variety of occupations. He worked for Lloyds Bank from 1917 to 1925, dealing with their foreign accounts, but also found time to indulge his passion for more literary pursuits. He wrote poetry, edited a literary magazine and was employed as a critic by the publishing giant Faber & Faber where he eventually became a director. His first marriage was not a particularly happy one as both he and his wife passed through varying degrees of emotional crises. At one point, in 1921, he and his wife moved out of London and spent some time in Margate where, his doctors hoped, the bracing sea air would help him recover from the nervous exhaustion from which he was

*The shelter in Margate where Eliot wrote part of 'The Waste Land' . . .*

*. . . and the view he would have had as he gazed out to sea.*

suffering. It was during this stay that he would sit and stare out into the distance from a seaside shelter on Margate front and give full rein to his thoughts, problems and anxieties. The result was at least part of what is now recognised as one of the most important poems in the whole canon of modern English poetry: 'The Waste Land' (1922). This strange, modernist poem is full of fragmentary sections and unexpected, obscure allusions, all held together by underlying feelings of gloom and pessimism. The title is thought to refer to Europe after the First World War but can no doubt be attributed partially to his own state of mind at the time. His other major work with Kent associations is *Murder in the Cathedral* (1935), a verse play based on the murder of Thomas à Becket in Canterbury Cathedral.

Eliot's contribution to not just English literature but to world literature cannot be overestimated. Works such as *The Love Song of Alfred J. Prufrock* (1917) and *The Four Quartets* (1935–42), as well as a host of philosophical writings and works of criticism ensured him a place among the greats and earned him the Nobel Prize for Literature in 1948.

# 5

# MOVERS & SHAKERS

Kent, like most counties, has had its share of people who have made a difference. In almost all walks of human activity, ranging from science to fashion or sport to medicine, there is no shortage of people who made a unique contribution to, and achieved greatness in, their chosen field and who were either born in Kent or chose to make the county their home.

## SCIENCE

One of the greatest thinkers of all time, **Charles Darwin (1809–82)**, lived at Down House, in the village of Downe near Orpington, for the last forty years of his life. It was in Down House that he wrote his major work *On the Origin of Species*, a book which caused outrage among traditional Christians as it turned the teachings of the Bible on their head.

Darwin was born in Shrewsbury and was originally destined for a medical career and so studied medicine at Edinburgh University. But he was not cut out to be a doctor and so he upped sticks and moved to Cambridge where he enrolled as a theology student in 1828 with a view to entering the Church. But his passion for natural history meant that he spent more time gathering interesting specimens than studying divinity. He managed to graduate, but after a time spent exploring the fauna and flora of North Wales, he was invited by the Royal Navy to join HMS *Beagle* on a voyage around the world as the ship's naturalist and this was to be the making of him. Had he not received the invitation he might have lived the unspectacular life of an obscure village parson, but the observations he made on his travels, and the conclusions he drew from them, changed not only the path of his career but the way we now view the world. When he reached the Galapagos Islands he discovered a world which had remained unchanged for millions of years and life forms which, although related, had evolved to suit different habitats. Finches, he noted in particular, had evolved different shaped beaks to fit in with the different conditions on the various islands. The two main conclusions that he arrived at were (i) all creatures are related and have a common ancestor and (ii) those which don't adapt to their surroundings perish. Of course all this brought him into direct conflict with the established Church. For centuries religious doctrine had taught that God created the world in six days and on the seventh rested. It also taught that God created everything on Earth and had created Man in his own image. But Darwin, with his theories of evolution and natural selection, cast serious doubt on such beliefs. For him the scientific evidence was convincing proof that the Earth, plants and animals (including Man) had evolved over millions of years from primitive life forms. When he published his findings he was attacked and ridiculed by the religious establishment, but gradually his ideas came to be accepted by the scientific community. Acceptance, however, was never absolute and even today the controversy smoulders on throughout the world. There are many traditionalists who still regard Darwin's ideas as sacrilege and blasphemy.

## MEDICINE

Towards the end of the sixteenth century an event was to take place which eventually led to an enormous leap in Man's understanding of his own body. In the little town of Folkestone the merchant Thomas Harvey and his wife became the proud parents of a boy who grew up to be one of the most important figures in the history of medicine. William Harvey (1578–1657) was educated at King's School, Canterbury, and then went on to study at Cambridge University. This was followed by a period of study at Padua University in Italy where the young William came into contact with one of the leading medical researchers

*The William Harvey statue in Folkestone.*

of the day: Hieronymus Fabricius. He had long been fascinated by anatomy and so infectious was his enthusiasm for his subject that he was soon able to pass his passion on to the young student from England. In particular Fabricius had noticed that inside all creatures there is a sophisticated and complicated network of blood vessels that seem to carry blood around the whole body. But he was somewhat foxed by the presence of valves at various points which seemed to either restrict or regulate the flow of blood. It took William and his dogged persistence to get to the bottom of the puzzle to come up with the answer and, in 1628, he published his major work *Exercitatio Anatomica de Motu Cordis et Sanguinis in Animalibus* ('An anatomical study of the motion of the heart and of blood in animals). In this work he explained the relationship between the blood vessels and the heart: the heart pumped blood in a circular direction around the body and the valves made sure that the blood did not flow the wrong way. All this might seem obvious to us in the twenty-first century, but in the seventeenth it was an astounding, revolutionary discovery. Without an understanding of how and why the blood circulates around the body, medicine could not have progressed to the giddy heights of knowledge and understanding we enjoy today. In 1645 he was appointed Warden of Merton College, Oxford, where he was able to shut himself away (despite being physician to King Charles I) from the turmoil of the Civil War and bury himself in his books and research. Three of his brothers and his wife predeceased him and his remaining days were spent visiting his two surviving brothers. One of them lived at Roehampton and it was during a visit there that William died on 3 June 1657.

## PRINTING

It seems hard to credit it but the crude, labour-intensive machine we now think of as the first printing press was the ancestor of the modern word-processor. And it is even harder to credit that the printing presses which were used throughout the world right up to 1980s were essentially the same design as those used in the fifteenth century. But when **William Caxton (*c.* 1422–92)** introduced what passed then for new technology into England its effect was earth-shattering. All of a sudden books appeared and made knowledge and ideas available on a scale which had not even been dreamed of before.

Not a lot is known about the man who made all this possible. He was born in about 1422 somewhere in Kent and probably in the Tenterden area. At the age of sixteen he was apprenticed to a rich London wool merchant, Robert Large, and then spent a large part of his adult life travelling around, and living in, Europe. He became fluent in French and Dutch, moved in quite elevated social circles and, from 1462 to 1470, did a stint as governor the English Nation of Merchant Adventurers (English wool merchants who traded with their counterparts from the Low Countries). On one of his trips to Cologne he encountered the printing press, recently invented by Johannes Gutenberg. He immediately spotted the potential for such new-fangled technology and set about mastering the art of printing. On his return to Bruges, where he was living at the time, he collaborated with a Flemish calligrapher, Colard Mansion, to produce the first book ever printed in English, *The Recuyell* [story] *of the History of Troye* (1473). Then, in 1476, he returned to England and established a printing works in Westminster. Among the many works he printed were Chaucer's *Canterbury Tales,* Gower's *Confessio Amantis* (*A Lover's Confession*) and Malory's *Le Morte d'Arthur.*

## POLITICS

One of the greatest of all the 'movers and shakers' in British history has to be **Sir Winston Churchill**. A measure of his greatness can be garnered from the fact that if he had not shown such bulldog tenacity and resistance to Hitler from 1939 to 1945 I would probably now be writing this in German. Many people in this country and throughout the world had given up all hope of our not capitulating to the Nazis and it was mainly Churchill who was responsible for Britain's survival.

Winston Leonard Spencer-Churchill (1874–1965) was born in Blenheim Palace, the son of a prominent Tory politician and an American heiress. He was educated at Harrow and Sandhurst before embarking on what was to be a glorious military career. Never one to dodge the bullets, Winston saw action in India, the Sudan and in South Africa where he was captured by the Boers, but made a daring escape. On his return to England he took up politics and became Tory MP for Oldham in 1900. However, he had a serious disagreement with the Conservative Party and joined the Liberals in 1904, no doubt helping them to their electoral victory in 1905. He held several cabinet posts and in 1911 was appointed First Lord of the Admiralty, a post he was forced to resign a few years later after the First World War fiasco of the Dardanelles. At this point he rejoined the army and saw action on the Western Front, but by 1917 was back in government, this time as Minister for Munitions. Things, however, were not so good for him in the 1930s and he found himself very much out of favour with all sides of the political spectrum because of three factors: he supported the king during

the abdication crisis, he vehemently opposed independence for India and he warned about the dangers of German rearmament and the rise of National Socialism at a time when most politicians preferred to turn a blind eye to the problem.

In addition to being a soldier and politician Churchill was also an accomplished painter and a prolific writer and much of his creative side found expression when he ensconced himself in Chartwell, his family home from 1922 until his death in 1965, tucked away deep in the Kent countryside. He wrote many books, but those for which he is best known are *A History of the English-Speaking Peoples* (1956–8) and *The Second World War* (1948–53). He was awarded the Nobel Prize for Literature in 1953.

A genuine 'Man of Kent' politician was **Sir Edward Heath** whose conviction that the best way to secure lasting peace in Europe and greater economic prosperity for the whole country was for

Britain to forge strong economic links with the rest of Europe. He was born in 1916 in Broadstairs, the son of a carpenter and a maid. He demonstrated a precocious gift for music and was an accomplished pianist and organist by his early teens. At Chatham House Grammar School he also displayed other academic ability and eventually won a place at Balliol College, Oxford, where he studied Politics, Philosophy and Economics. During his time at Oxford he also won an organ scholarship and this allowed him to stay on a university for an extra year. While at university his interest in politics continued to grow and, as President of the university Conservative Association, he adopted a markedly anti-appeasement stance as the clouds of war were gathering over Europe. He visited Spain during the Civil War and was in Germany just weeks before the outbreak of the Second World War. At a Nazi rally (purely as an observer) he famously rubbed shoulders, quite literally, with Adolf Hitler and was introduced to several of the Nazi leaders, including Heinrich Himmler whom he subsequently described as the most evil man he had ever met. After the war Heath embarked on a variety of careers before finally settling on being a politician and winning the Bexley seat in 1950. As President of the Board of Trade (1963–4) he did much of the groundwork for taking Britain into the Common Market (as the European Union was then known), a move which was finally completed in 1973 when he was Prime Minister. It was also during Heath's Premiership that Britain abandoned its age-old coinage system (pounds, shillings and pence) and adopted the decimal system we use today. After a long career in politics Edward Heath died at his home in Salisbury, Wiltshire, in 2005.

# FASHION

You don't have to be a dedicated follower of fashion to know the name **Zandra Rhodes**, a designer whose effect on the post-war fashion scene is almost incalculable. The drab uniformity and conformity of the late 1940s and early '50s had been shaken a bit in the Teddy Boy era, followed by Italian suits for the boys and hooped skirts for the girls. But then came the sartorial tsunami of the 1960s, driven by a Kentish Maid whose impact on clothing, hairstyles and even furniture is still with us today. **Zandra (Lindsey) Rhodes CBE, RDI,** was born in Chatham in 1940 and from a very early age was exposed to the mystique of clothes design as her mother was both a fitter for a Paris couturier and a lecturer in design at the Medway College of Art. It was at this college that Zandra began her serious studies in fashion before progressing to the Royal College of Art in London. Although she was obviously gifted in all aspects of art and design as applied to fashion, she made printed textile design her specialism. Characteristic of all her work is her emphasis on colour; not the subdued contrasts of pastel shades, but bright, shocking juxtapositions of reds, greens and yellows which, we might add, are reflected in her own hairstyles. In her youth she went in for tinting her hair bright green but now, with greater maturity, has settled on a rather garish pink. In 1966 she made the move from the purely academic side of design into the commercial, co-owning a boutique in London. A few years later she decided to go solo and opened her own outlet on the Fulham Road in the fashionable area of South Kensington. If there had been any doubts about her future success in her chosen field up to this date they were well and truly dissipated now. Her career progressed on an upward curve and has still, some would argue, not yet reached its apex. In November 2009 she was appointed first Chancellor of the University for the Creative Arts.

# SPORT

One of the most successful and colourful characters in the history of British sport, few would deny, was the boxing legend **Sir Henry Cooper.** 'Our 'Enery', as he was affectionately known, was born in London in 1934 and grew up in a less than affluent area of the capital where the ability to defend oneself was a necessary skill. He was one of three sons, and during the London Blitz they were evacuated to Lancing in Sussex ('right into the flight-path of the German bombers' Henry was to quip later on) along with hundreds of other children for whom London was considered far too dangerous. The three brothers all demonstrated an early flair and ability for football and cricket, but it was as a boxer that Henry was to make his mark. He represented England in the 1952

Olympics and held the British Heavyweight title for over ten years. After turning professional he went on to fight some of the best boxers in the world but is probably most famously remembered as the first man to floor the amazingly skilled American boxer Cassius Clay (later known as Muhammad Ali) in 1963 when he caught him with a powerful upper cut in the fourth round and sent him sprawling against the bottom rope. Everyone thought that the contest was over but a badly cut eye meant that Cooper had to concede defeat and Clay was saved from humiliation. Henry also went on to become the first boxer ever to win the Lonsdale Belt three times and was also named BBC Sports Personality of the Year twice – in 1967 and 1970. He retired from the ring in 1971 after losing on points to the up-and-coming Joe Bugner. Cooper, who was knighted in 2000, lived in Hildenborough, Kent, where he was the Chairman of the Nizels golf club. He sadly passed away in 2011.

Another sportsman of exceptional note associated with Kent is **Michael Colin Cowdrey (1932–2000)**. Although he was born in India, he can rightly be claimed as one of the county's most famous sons, if only by adoption. He was sent to England by his parents from India in 1946 where he enrolled as a boarder at Tonbridge School. Within a very short time after settling in he demonstrated outstanding ability as a cricketer; he was a formidable batsman and no mean bowler, with a devastating leg-break delivery which left many an opposing batsman awestruck. In 1950 he was appointed Head of School and, in the same year, he made his first appearance as a member of the Kent cricket team. In 1951 he went up to Oxford and captained the university team in 1954, the same year that Len Hutton included him in the England team as it prepared for the MCC tour of Australia. The trip turned out to be a watershed in Cowdrey's life; not only did he help England win the Ashes but he also decided that the world of academe was not for him and he would be a professional cricketer for as long as the game wanted him. As it turned out the cricketing world needed him for a long time. He played for England for the next fifteen years and, from 1957 to 1971, also captained Kent. He was the first cricketer to play in 100 Test matches and scored a record-breaking total 7,624 runs for England. The years finally caught up with him and decided that it was time to retire in 1975, but his association with the game he loved continued as he moved over to the administrative side of the sport. He was knighted in 1992 and elevated to the peerage in 1997 adopting the title Lord Cowdrey of Tonbridge. In 2000 he suffered a fatal heart attack and the world of cricket was robbed of one of its greatest ever exponents. He was sadly missed, not only by the cricketing fraternity, but by the nation as a whole.

## TELEVISION

You would have to had been born on a distant planet not to know the name of one of the most dynamic personalities to dominate British television since the 1960s, **Sir David Paradine Frost**. He was born in Tenterden in 1939, the son of a Methodist minister. The family moved to Gillingham while David was still a boy and he began his formal education at Gillingham Grammar School, before going up to Gonville and Caius College, Cambridge, where he read English. The family did entertain the idea of his following in his father's footsteps and entering the Church, but David had other ideas. On graduating he took up a traineeship with Associated Rediffusion (an independent broadcasting company) and Anglia Television. For most people who remember the 1960s David Frost hit the big time in 1963 when he fronted *That Was the Week that Was*, a satirical programme, the like of which had never been seen before on British television. Almost overnight it became a cult show and compulsive viewing for the whole country. Anybody who was anybody could find themselves being lampooned by the team (David Frost, Willie Rushton, Lance Percival and Millicent Martin). This was fine if you were one of the millions of viewers, but the politicians who frequently found themselves on the receiving end of the show's characteristic acerbic satire took a different view. On one famous occasion Bernard Levin, an acid-tongued critic who frequently appeared with the rest of the team, was punched on air by an irate member of the public who took exception to remarks Levin had made about his wife.

After the demise of the show, David Frost's star did not wane. He went on to host a seeming endless number of other shows both in Britain and the United States. The hallmark of his programmes was his searching questioning technique and he interviewed all the leading politicians of the day, famously grilling the shamed and discredited Richard Nixon, the President of the United States whose political career was ended ignominiously after the Watergate Affair. Sir David then went on to host the Sunday morning current affairs programme *Breakfast with Frost*, which ran from 1993 to 2005.

Had it not been for a certain ex-pat Scot who spent some time in Kent, Sir David might never have been in a position to make a career out of television. **John Logie Baird (1888–1946)** was born in Helensburgh, Scotland, the son of a clergyman. He studied engineering at Glasgow University and, rejected by the army during the First World War owing to ill health, he decided to set himself up in business. In 1924 he moved to Folkestone and worked with the electrical and radio engineering firm of T.C. Gilbert & Co, of 26 Guildhall Street. It was on these premises that he conducted his early experiments into the transmission of images and it was from these tiny first steps that the wonder of modern television emerged.

# MUSIC

Ask anybody who knows anything at all about music to name the foremost British conductors of the age and they will almost certainly mention the giants such as Sir Thomas Beecham, Sir John Barbirolli and, of course, 'Flash Harry', otherwise known as Sir Malcolm Sargent. **Harold Malcolm Watts Sargent (1895–1967)** was born in Ashford, the son of a coal merchant, but was brought up in Stamford, Lincolnshire. While still a young child he showed the unmistakable signs of being musically gifted, taking to the piano as the proverbial duck takes to water, and was soon accepted as a chorister in Peterborough Cathedral. Soon after this he won an organ scholarship at Stamford School, where his early talent now bloomed so that by the tender age of fourteen he was accompanying school productions such as Gilbert and Sullivan's *The Yeomen of the Guard* and *The Gondoliers*. By the time he was sixteen he was an Associate of the Royal College of Organists and at eighteen was awarded the degree of Bachelor of Music by Durham University. In 1914, when he was no more than nineteen years old, he became the organist for St Mary's Church in Melton Mowbray, Leicestershire, a post which he held for the next ten years (apart from eight months in the Durham Light Infantry during the First World War). As if all this were not enough, recognition of his talent and honours just followed Malcolm Sargent around and when he was just twenty-four he was awarded a Doctorate of Music by Durham University and became the youngest ever holder of the degree in England. As his career progressed he forged associations with the leading musical companies, not just in Britain, but throughout the world. His CV would have glowed with impressive references to Ballets Russes, the Royal Choral Society, the D'Oyly Carte Opera Company, the London and Liverpool Philharmonics, the Royal Philharmonic, the BBC Symphony Orchestra, etc. He was also passionate about bringing music to the people as opposed to reserving it for the élite. But this did not mean that he 'dumbed down' in any sense; he set very high standards among his fellow musicians and in fact fell out of favour with some of them at one point in his career. During an interview in 1936 he famously stated that he did not believe musicians should be entitled to a job for life. On the contrary, he believed a musician should sweat blood at every performance and think that his very future depended upon it. At the beginning of the Second World War, while in Australia, he was offered a prestigious musical directorship but turned it down. Rather than accept, he returned to Britain to 'do his bit' for the war effort by using music to boost the morale of the British public as they faced Hitler's onslaught. In 1948 he took over from Sir Henry Wood as Chief Conductor of the Proms, a position he held until his death in 1967. Throughout his life he was a close friend of Sir Thomas Beecham, even though he was frequently on the receiving end of his bitingly sarcastic wit. When Beecham heard that 'Flash Harry' had been shot at during a visit to Palestine he is reported to have quipped, 'I had no idea the Arabs were so musical.'

A Kentish Man and musician of a very different ilk is **Mick Jagger**. He was born in Dartford in 1943 where his father was a schoolteacher and his mother a hairdresser. Michael was a bright lad at school and passed the 11+ exam to go on to Dartford Grammar School, leaving a few years later with a respectable clutch of O levels and three A levels. By his own admission he went into the entertainment business because, when he looked around him, such a move would give him the best chance of making the 'kind of bread' (i.e. money) that he wanted. Fortunately for him, his financial ambitions were matched by a certain talent for music and an even greater talent for the kind of lifestyle which would bring him fame, notoriety and the kind of wealth that accompanies outrageous celebrity behaviour. He burst onto the pop scene in 1962 as the lead singer of the Rolling Stones (with Bill Wyman, Keith Richards and Brian Jones – Charlie Watts joined the group in 1963). The group's style has generally been described as 'counter culture' as their antics, on and off stage, have always been somewhat anarchic and rebellious. In the early days they were frequently in the press because of their run-ins with the police and other representatives of the establishment and Mick is almost as famous for his relationships as he is for his music. The list of his ladyfriends is almost endless and he fathered no fewer than seven children with four women. But despite his refusal to conform he was knighted in 2003 'for services to music'. Even the most conservative echelons of society had recognised that Mick Jagger and the Rolling Stones had brought something original to the cultural scene of late twentieth-century Britain. Furthermore, their record sales alone had contributed much appreciated revenue to the Chancellor's coffers at a time when the country was strapped for cash and 'all contributions were gratefully received'.

# ART

She is not everybody's cup of tea, but there is no getting away from the fact that **Tracey Karima Emin RA** has had a traumatic effect on the art world. She was born in Croydon in 1963 but was brought up in Margate where her Turkish Cypriot father owned a hotel. She achieved fame (some might say infamy) for her surprising, if not shocking, works of art. Pretty landscapes, awe-inspiring sunsets and the like, the more traditional subjects for painters and artists, are not to be found in her works. She is more interested in turning intensely personal thoughts, emotions and experiences into creations which are intended to be seen as works of art. The results are not always what everybody would term 'art' but there are enough people who claim to understand art for her to have achieved status in that world. Her subject matter (rape, sex, abortion, etc.) which at one time would have been consigned to the world of pornography, has found acceptance among those who claim to be able to see beneath the surface of her work and appreciate the emotional stimuli which form the basis of her work. Famously the unmade bed, entitled simply 'My Bed', aroused mixed responses when it was entered for the Turner Prize in 1999. To many it was nothing more than an unmade bed, but others saw it as a wonderfully constructed symbol of the artist's life of sexual excess, sensuality and self-neglect. Another work, 'Everybody I have ever slept with 1963–95', is little more than a tent with the names of all the people she has occupied a bed with embroidered onto the canvas. When it was first shown it was interpreted as a colourfully displayed list of her lovers, but in fact the names include family members with whom she innocently enjoyed the warm security of a cuddle-up in a cosy bed when she was a child. The tent was destroyed in a fire in 2004.

Tracey Emin studied at the Medway College of Design between 1980 and 1982 and in 1987 was awarded an MA by the Royal College of Art. She then went on to study philosophy at Birkbeck College, University of London. Her talent and originality achieved official recognition when she was appointed Royal Academician in 2007.

A perhaps lesser known side to Ms Emin is the work she does for charity. She has raised thousands of pounds for Sir Elton John's AIDS Foundation and has also given generously to women and children in Africa who are affected by HIV/AIDS.

## JOURNALISM

**Bill Deedes** (or the Right Honourable the Lord Deedes KBE, MC, PC, DL to give him his official title) made a contribution to journalism which was second to none. He was widely recognised as the finest journalist of his day and by the time of his death he had been involved in the profession for over seventy-six years. Bill, as he liked to be addressed, was known among his colleagues for his gentlemanly manner, his keen mind and gentle (never malicious) sarcasm. He walked and talked with royalty, edited a major newspaper and was a Member of Parliament for almost twenty-five years and yet he never lost the common touch. He would travel from Ashford to London in a standard class compartment and enjoyed nothing so much as chatting with his fellow travellers. And he would express his opinions on just about anything from the latest earthquake in India to the situation in Rwanda or the fact that there was as yet no platform buffet on the newly opened Ashford International station.

William Francis Deedes was born in 1913 in Kent and was brought up in Saltwood Castle near Hythe. He was educated at Harrow School and probably would have gone on to a glittering university career, had it not been for a serious downturn in the family fortunes. Bill's father lost an enormous amount of money in the 1929 Wall Street Crash and so the prospect of a university education for young William disappeared virtually overnight. But the university's loss turned out to be journalism's gain as, in 1931, the future editor and MP set out on what was to be a life-long association with one of the most respected and influential newspapers in the country. He first became a junior reporter on the *Morning Post* and then was absorbed along with the paper into the *Daily Telegraph* in 1937. At the tender age of twenty-two he was sent off by his editor to cover the war in Abyssinia where his sharp eye and journalistic instinct meant that, despite his lack of years, his reputation as one of the country's finest journalists was assured. He had a flair for language and ability to express himself in the clear lucid prose which was the envy of many of his colleagues. He did have a tendency to mix up his metaphors occasionally but this was regarded as a charming eccentricity rather than a defect in his skill as a writer.

According to those who knew him, he could be a bit of a shambles at times and his contemporary Evelyn Waugh is thought to have based his fictional character, William Boot, on him in his satirical novel *Scoop*.

In 1974 Bill Deedes accepted the post of editor of the *Daily Telegraph* and carried out his onerous duties (briefly at the same time as representing his Ashford constituency in Westminster) with aplomb. He is the only person in history to have both held ministerial office in the government and been the editor of a national newspaper.

When he decided in 1986 that it was time to hand over the ever more demanding duties of an editor to a younger man (Sir Max Hastings) it was by no means a signal that he wished to retire to Kent and grow vegetables. He continued to write for the newspaper that had been so much a part of his life and entertained his readers with wittily observant comments on politics and world events. But he also usually found time to end his column with a homely description of the Kentish countryside or some issue of local, as opposed to national, importance. He would describe his garden draped in the first ethereal mists of autumn, effuse over the early blooms he had spotted in spring, or express his despair at the way local teachers had been priced out of the housing market by the spiralling property prices.

When he died in 2007 the obituaries were generous and laudatory, and a frequently repeated sentiment was the cliché that we would not see his like in our lifetime again. But in his case it was true.

# 6

# OUT & ABOUT IN KENT

## PLACES IN KENT AND THEIR MOTTOES

| | |
|---|---|
| Kent County Council | Invicta (Unconquered) |
| Ashford Borough Council | With stronger faith |
| Canterbury City Council | Ave Mater Angliae (Hail Mother of England) |
| Dartford Borough Council | Floreat Dartford (Let Dartford flourish) formerly:Tenax et Fidelis (steadfast and faithful) |
| Maidstone Borough Council | Agriculture and commerce |
| Medway Unitary Authority | Forward together |
| Shepway District Council | Amoenitas et salubritas (Charm and health) |
| Swale Borough Council | Known by their fruits |
| Tonbridge and Malling Borough Council | Forward in Unison |
| Tunbridge Wells Borough Council | Do well and doubt not |
| Sevenoaks Town Council | Floreant septem quercus (Let seven oaks flourish) |
| Southborough Town Council | Propia tuemur (We look after our own) |
| Chatham Borough Council | Loyal and true |
| Gillingham Borough Council | With Fort and Fleet for Home and England |
| Rochester upon Medway City Council | Loyal and True |

| | |
|---|---|
| Sittingbourne and Milton Urban District Council | Known by their Fruits |
| Strood Rural District Council | Spes patriae rus (the hope of the nation is in the countryside) |

## WHAT THE ROMANS CALLED THEM

| | |
|---|---|
| Canterbury | Durovernum Cantiacorum |
| Rochester | Durobrivae |
| Springhead | Vagniacae |
| Crayford | Noviomagus |
| Reculver | Regulbium |
| Richborough | Rutupiae |
| Dover | Portus Dubris |
| Lympne | Portus Lemanis |
| Isle of Thanet | Tanatus Insula |
| South Foreland | Cantium Promontorium |
| River Thames | Tamesis flumen |
| Faversham | Durolevum |

## SOME FAMOUS PEOPLE BURIED IN CANTERBURY CATHEDRAL

**St Alphege (d. 1012)** Archbishop of Canterbury captured and killed by the Danes

**St Anslem (1033–1109)** Archbishop and thought to be the founder of Scholasticism

**Thomas Arundel (1353–1414)** Archbishop who clashed with Wycliffe and the Lollards

**Edward (1330–76)** also known as the Black Prince

**Orlando Gibbons (1583–1625)** Foremost composer and organist of his times

**Henry IV (1366–1413)** thought to have died in Canterbury of leprosy

**Joan of Navarre (1370–1437)** the second wife of Henry IV

**Somerset Maugham (1874–1965)** author. His ashes are scattered in the cathedral grounds

## TOWNS & CITIES,
## SOME FACTS & STATS

*Canterbury*

| | |
|---|---|
| Population | 44,000 (approx) |
| River | the Stour |
| Dialling code | 01227 |

The modern name is a contraction of Cantwareburgh, literally, the 'stronghold' (burgh) of 'the men' (ware) of Kent. But we have already seen that Kent takes its name from the Celtic for 'edge' so the origin of the city's name is really 'the stronghold of the men of the edge'. Originally an Iron Age settlement, Canterbury was developed by the Romans but then was taken over by the Anglo-Saxons when the Roman legions departed. It soon became

*A surviving part of Canterbury's defensive walls. Known as the West Gate this is thought to be one of the first structures in England modified to be defended with firearms as opposed to bow and arrow.*

*The entrance to Canterbury Cathedral.*

a centre of learning after St Augustine made it the centre of Christianity in England. It is still the principal see of the Church of England and Canterbury Cathedral is a world heritage site. The city was badly bombed during the Second World War as part of the 'Baedeker raids', the air raids on towns and cities throughout Britain which featured in the pre-war tourist guidebook published by the German publisher Karl Baedeker.

Canterbury Cathedral is also remembered for the murder of Thomas Becket (also known as Thomas à Becket), 29 December 1170, supposedly on the orders of Henry II who is thought to have bemoaned 'who will rid me of this turbulent priest?' The story of the murder was turned into the play *Murder in the Cathedral* by T.S. Eliot (first performed 1935).

The university, officially designated the University of Kent at Canterbury, was inaugurated in 1965. Famous alumni include: Kazuo Ishiguro (author), Gavin Esler (BBC correspondent), Rosie Boycott (journalist), Alan Davies (actor), Mark Mardell (BBC correspondent), Sir Hugh Orde (former Chief Constable of Northern Ireland), Tom Wilkinson (actor), Carolyn Quinn (BBC correspondent) and Paul Ross (TV presenter).

## Dover

| | |
|---|---|
| Population | 29,000 (approx.) |
| River | the Dour |
| Dialling code | 01304 |

Dover is an ancient town and has always been thought of as the gateway to England. It takes its name from *dubro* the Celtic for 'water,' which is also the origin of the name of the river on which the town stands. The famous white cliffs (immortalised by Vera Lynn) gave Britain its other ancient name: Albion, a name derived from the Latin 'albus', meaning white. (In fact 'albus' meant 'dull white' as opposed to 'candidus' which was 'brilliant white'.) Archaeological evidence is pretty clear that there was a settlement in the area during the Stone Age. The Domesday Book devotes quite a lot of space to Dover, as it was already an important communications link for travel between London, Canterbury and Continental Europe. During the Second World War it played a vital role, both as a point of embarkation for British troops and as a link in the defensive chain along the south coast. Its passenger sailings were seriously curtailed when the Channel Tunnel was built, but three ferry companies still operate out of the port: P&O Ferries (Dover–Calais), SeaFrance (Dover–Calais) and DFDS Seaways (Dover–Dunkirk).

Famous people associated with Dover include Simon Cowell, the entrepreneur, who was a student at the public school Dover College. The politician and novelist Geoffrey Archer taught Physical Education at the same school in the 1960s. Joss Stone, the blues singer and songwriter, was born in Dover in 1987.

## Maidstone

| | |
|---|---|
| Population: | 139,000 (approx.) |
| River | the Medway |
| Dialling code: | 01622 |

Now the county town of Kent, it takes its name from the Saxon *maegden stan* (maiden stone) although nobody has come up with a definitive explanation as to why the place should be named in honour of a girl (or girls) and a stone (or stones). One suggestion is that this was a meeting place of sorts where the young women of the area washed their menfolk's clothes in the river and then spread them out on the stones to dry. This does, however, smack of pop. etymology and another explanation, that it was a place where young girls gathered for some religious purposes, has more of the ring of plausibility about it. Yet another possibility, however, is that this is where young nubile ladies would gather to be inspected by prospective husbands in the dim and distant past when such behaviour would not have been considered politically incorrect. But so far these are all just theories.

During the English Civil War Maidstone sided with the Parliamentarian cause and it was the mayor, Andrew Broughton, who signed the warrant for the execution of Charles I. In more recent times the town has taken advantage of its position and developed into a major distribution centre for the various industries that were established locally. Its proximity to both London and the coast, at the centre of an excellent communications network, has always meant that it was an ideal place for industrial development. Traditionally, brewing, paper production, quarrying and cloth manufacturing were important industries in the region, although these have tended to decline in recent years.

Famous people associated with Maidstone include Ann Widdecombe (MP for Maidstone 1987–2010), James Burke (TV presenter) who attended Maidstone Grammar school, Shaun Williamson (actor) who attended St Simon Stock School and Tony Hart (artist and TV presenter) who was born in Maidstone in 1925.

## Ramsgate

| | |
|---|---|
| Population | 40, 000 (approx.) |
| Dialling code | 01843 |

Ramsgate began life as a tiny hamlet making a living from fishing and farming. It takes its name from the Anglo-Saxon *hraefen* (raven) and *geat* (a gap between cliffs). Exactly what the reference to a raven is remains unclear; possibly a nearby rock was shaped in such a way that it reminded someone of a raven or possibly 'raven' was just somebody's nickname. The most important feature of the town is the harbour, the construction of which began in 1749 and was completed in 1850. It is the only harbour in the whole of the country to be officially designated as a Royal Harbour. The Victorians 'discovered' Ramsgate in the nineteenth century when they began flocking there in their hundreds after hearing

*Queen Victoria loved Ramsgate and often holidayed there.*

how beneficial sea-bathing was for one's health. Its popularity has declined somewhat over the years but it has a magnificent marina which is one of the biggest on the south coast of England.

Famous people associated with Ramsgate include Brenda Blethyn (actress) who has a house in the town and John le Mesurier (actor) who is buried there. Queen Victoria liked the place so much she frequently used it as a holiday destination.

## Faversham

| | |
|---|---|
| Population | 18,000 (approx) |
| Dialling code | 01795 |

Faversham is one of the oldest and, many say, prettiest of the towns and cities in Kent. It also has some of the closest ties with royalty as it owes its existence in no small measure to one of England's earliest monarchs: King Stephen (r. 1135–54). It was he who founded an abbey at Faversham (the abbey no longer exists and the site is now occupied by Queen Elizabeth's Grammar School) in the twelfth century and thus lent the town a certain regal status (it was briefly the capital of England) which it maintained for centuries. Stephen, his wife Matilda of Boulogne and son Prince Eustace are all buried there.

There was a settlement in the area in pre-Roman times, although its name suggests that when the Saxons and Jutes arrived it was already gaining something of a reputation for the metalworking skills of the locals. The Domesday Book records the settlement as Favreshant, but this is almost certainly a Norman corruption of the version recorded in 811 as Fevresham, from the Anglo-Saxon *faefor* meaning 'smith' or 'metalworker' and *ham* meaning 'homestead'. Obviously, the presence of at least an embryonic metalworking industry as early as the ninth century cannot be ruled out.

For much of its history (actually from the sixteenth century) Faversham was associated with the manufacture of gunpowder. Its position for such an industry was ideal: situated as it is on the coast the gunpowder could be easily exported, and as it was close to the Weald of Kent there was a plentiful supply of trees and timber to provide the charcoal, one of the main ingredients of gunpowder. It was also, because of the town's coastal position, easy for sulphur (another essential ingredient) to be imported from abroad. But the town's explosives history has not been without mishap. There were several serious incidents over the years when either carelessness or ignorance led to catastrophic explosions resulting in serious injury and loss of life. In 1934 some bright spark (pardon the pun!) realised that in any future war aircraft would play a leading role and Faversham's proximity to Europe would leave its explosives industry vulnerable to attack. It was therefore decided to move the facility to Scotland. Looking back, it seems like a wise move.

Faversham's other industry is brewing and the town claims to have one of the oldest breweries in Britain, Shepherd Neame, named after Percy Beale Neame (1836–1913) who amalgamated the family brewery with the Shepherd and Mares brewery and became the sole proprietor in 1877.

Perhaps the two most interesting former residents of the town are saints Crispin and Crispianus who, after fleeing persecution in Rome, are thought to have lived and worked in Faversham from AD 284 to 286. The story is that they worked as cobblers on or near the site of the Swan Inn on today's Market Street where there is a plaque that reads: 'Near to this house dwelt saints Crispin and Crispianus, the patron saints of bootmakers', though the plaque makes no mention of the fact that Crispin and Crispianus are also the patron saints of saddlemakers. St Crispin has his saint's day on 25 October.

## Gravesend

| | |
|---|---|
| Population | 56,000 (approx) |
| River | Thames |
| Dialling code | 01474 |

The town's less than reassuring name is rather unfortunate. The apparent association with our eventual passing is just that – apparent. The town has no more association with graveyards than any other as the 'grave' in this case is the Anglo-Saxon *grafe* meaning woodland grove or thicket. The Domesday Book referred to it as Gravesham (homestead in the grove) and by 1157 it had become Gravessend –'the end of the grove'. Because of its position, shipping has always played a major role in the economy of the town, although more recently cement and paper production has also figured largely. One of the major features of the town today is its pier. At a time when piers generally are disappearing (or have disappeared) from other coastal towns, Gravesend renovated its 1834 pier in 2004 and it now boasts a restaurant and bar. One of the town's most interesting tourist attractions, however, is the statue in St George's churchyard of Pocahontas. Pocahontas (*c.* 1595–1617) was the daughter of a native American chief who married John Rolfe, an Englishman who had settled in Jamestown, Virginia. On her marriage and conversion to Christianity she adopted the name Rebecca and after a visit to England she and her husband made plans to go back home to the Americas. They boarded a ship in London but as it made its leisurely way down the Thames, Pocahontas was taken ill and had to be put ashore at Gravesend where she died at the age of about twenty-two. Rolfe and his wife had one son, born in 1615, who carried on the line so that their descendants can still be found today in Virginia and other parts of the USA. One such is Nancy Reagan, who was married to the late former President Ronald Reagan.

Other notables associated with Gravesend include the poet Thom Gunn, who was born in the town in 1929 and Gemma Arterton (actress) who was born there in 1986. General George Gordon (1833–85), also known as Gordon of Khartoum and Chinese Gordon, lived in the town between 1865 and 1871 when he was responsible for the construction and upkeep of the forts along the south bank of the Thames.

## Folkestone

| | |
|---|---|
| Population | 54,000 (approx) |
| Dialling code | 01303 |

Historically Folkestone was the centre for the 'hundred' of the Lathe of Shepway and hence hosted the 'moots' – ancient think-tank discussion groups. As these meetings tended to take place around a specifically designated stone or boulder, the tradition could hold the key to the origin of the town's name – *folc* (people's) *stan* (stone). Another suggestion is that Folkestone is a corruption of *Falca's stan*, but who exactly Falca was and what was the precise significance of his stone, nobody can say with any certainty. The Domesday Book spelling was *Fulchestan* and there were several spellings of the name until Lord Radnor, a major landowner in the area, made a request for the spelling to be standardised in the mid-nineteenth century. It was also about this time that the town began to expand. It had been little more than a coastal fishing village centred around the harbour since the Middle Ages, but its proximity to France made it a prime target for commercial expansion when the railways arrived on the scene. The South Eastern Railway Company transformed the town into its main packet-steamer station for traffic heading for the Continent in general and Boulogne in particular. It remained an important departure point for travellers until 1994 when the Channel Tunnel opened and made the port a less than viable commercial operation. Among the main social developments in recent years have been the expansion of the Creative Quarter and the opening of the university. The town also boasts the Leas Cliff Hall and the Quarterhouse for major theatrical and musical productions. Folkestone also hosts an annual literary festival and attracts writers and artists from all over the country.

Famous people associated with Folkestone include Arthur Brough (actor) born in 1905, who established the Folkestone Repertory Company in the 1920s where, after the war, actors such as Ann Stallybrass, Polly James and Trevor Bannister learned their trade. Arthur died in Folkestone in 1978. June Brown (alias Dot Cotton of *Eastenders*) owns two properties in the town. The most famous visitor, however, was King Edward VII who used the Grand Hotel for his discreet trysts with Alice Keppel. The hotel is still there with its 'Keppel's Bar'.

## Ashford

| | |
|---|---|
| Population | 60,000 (approx) |
| River | Great Stour |
| Dialling code | 01233 |

Situated just about as close to the centre of the Weald (Anglo-Saxon for 'forest') of Kent as it is possible to get, Ashford is an ancient market town dating from the ninth century. One theory is that an even older settlement in the area, Great Chart, was raided by the Danes and refugees fled and settled a few miles down the road in what we now know as Ashford. The name itself is derived from the Anglo-Saxon *aesc-sceat-ford* 'the ford by a copse of ash trees'. There is a parish church situated in the centre of the town which dates back to the thirteenth century and the market, established in the Middle Ages, still takes place every Saturday. Although the town has changed dramatically over the years there are still some half-timbered buildings in the centre to remind residents and visitors alike of Ashford's ancient heritage. In more recent times the essentially agricultural nature of the town changed with the advent of the railways in the nineteenth century. Its position meant that many of the lines running through Kent converged at Ashford and, as probably the most important centre of rail communication between the coast and London, it became a prime target for German bombers in the Second World War. But the town's significance as a railway hub increased enormously after 1994 when the Channel Tunnel was opened. The old station was entirely demolished to be replaced by a brand new steel and glass construction renamed as Ashford International and intended to service Eurotunnel trains hurtling between London, Paris and Brussels. But in 2007, when it was decided to make Ebbsfleet International the principal stop between London and the Continent, many services from Ashford were either severely curtailed or dropped altogether.

Another of the town's proud boasts used to be that it was the home of the British Army's Intelligence Corps. From the 1960s the corps was based at Templar Barracks where servicemen from the Army, Navy and Air Force (and many from foreign forces as well) attended courses in all aspects of military intelligence. One of its most famous students was Prince Andrew who attended a course in 1982 when he was a serving officer in the Royal Navy. But in 1997 the camp was decommissioned as it happened to be lying right on the route of the proposed new high-speed rail line.

Famous people with Ashford connections include Ray Dorset, the lead singer with the band Mungo Jerry, who was born in the town in 1946; John Wells (satirist) was born in Ashford in 1936 and Bob Holness (TV presenter) was born in South Africa in 1928 but his family moved to Ashford while he was still a boy. Malcolm Sargent (conductor) and Frederick Forsyth (writer) were both born in the town and the French philosopher Simone Weil, who was born in Paris in 1909, died in Ashford in 1943.

## Tenterden
Population        8,000 (approx.)
Dialling code    01580

With its quaint buildings and tree-lined main street, Tenterden has to be one of the most charming little towns in Kent. In Saxon times it must have been owned by people far over to the east of the county and the clue to this lies in the name. It was originally known as Tenet Waraden meaning 'the clearing in the forest (*den*) owned by the men (*ware*) of Thanet (*Tenet*)'. In the fourteenth century it began to grow from being what was probably no more than a little hamlet when it became the centre of the wool trade. King Edward III had banned the export of wool and attracted the dyers and weavers of Flanders to come over from the Continent to instruct the English in the art of clothmaking. The town is now a distance of some 10 miles from the sea, but at one time it was situated right on the coast as much of Romney Marsh was below sea level. Because of its coastal position it played a vital role in the defence of the realm, in return for which it was granted full exemption from taxation. But as the coastline changed in the fifteenth and sixteenth centuries the town's role in the coastal defences of the kingdom decreased.

Famous people associated with Tenterden include Ellen Terry (1847–1928) the leading female Shakespearean actress of her day, who lived and died in Small Hythe, a hamlet just outside the town. Sir Donald Sinden (born 1923) lives near the town and Sir David Frost was born there.

## Rochester
Population        27,000 (approx)
Dialling code    01634

Historically Rochester was second in importance only to Canterbury. In Celtic, pre-Roman times, Rochester was the administrative centre of the western half of the county for the Cantiaci people and Canterbury was the 'capital' of the eastern half. Over the centuries the settlement went through several name changes: the earliest spelling was Durobrivis, recorded in AD 730, followed by Dorobrevis in AD 844. Both of these spellings suggest that there was 'a bridge over the waters' but archaeologists have failed to find any sign of an early bridge and, if there was one, it had already disappeared by the time the Romans arrived. From the late eighth century the place is recorded as Hrofaescaestre, then Hrofescester (811), Rovescestre (1086) and finally the name appeared as Rochester in 1610. Many of the extant buildings in Rochester date back to the fourteenth century. The building known as Abdication House, situated on the High Street, is so called because it is where James II spent his last night as King of England (December 1688) before his abdication. Another house, in Crow Lane, is where Charles II was entertained (20 May 1660) on the eve of the Restoration and so, unsurprisingly, the building is known as Restoration House. Interestingly, this is the very building used by Dickens as a model for Satis House, the home of Miss Havisham in *Great Expectations*.

But one event in Rochester's history sets it apart for every other town or city in England. In 1998 the powers that be decided to merge the city of Rochester with Gillingham and Chatham to create the Medway Unitary Authority. Unfortunately the outgoing council simply forgot to appoint the largely symbolic and mainly ceremonial body of Charter Trustees to ensure that the city retained its status. This oversight meant that the city did not retain its status and so the City of Rochester was demoted to a town overnight. The mistake was not noticed until 2002.

Notable people associated with Rochester include Charles Dickens (author), Kelly Brook (actress), Sir Cloudesley Shovell (admiral), John Selwyn Gummer (politician), Dinsdale Landon (actor) and Richard Dadd (artist) as well as Russell and Sybil Thorndike, mentioned earlier.

## Royal Tunbridge Wells

Population        57,000 (approx)
Dialling code     01892

Long associated with 'true blue' Toryism, Tunbridge Wells is a picturesque and quintessentially English town nestling just on the Kent side of the Kent/Sussex border. There was a settlement in the area in the Iron Age and archaeological evidence suggests that there was also a hill fort there prior to the Roman occupation. But it was not until the seventeenth century that the town really began to expand and, if the legend is to be believed, its sudden growth spurt is down to one man. In 1606 a courtier at the Court of King James I, Lord North, was on a hunting trip in the area and drank some of the local spring water. To his great surprise he experienced a noticeable improvement in his health and began to tell his friends about it. Within a very short space of time London socialites had heard about the wonderful health-giving properties of the spring waters down in Kent and Tunbridge Wells became the place to be and to be seen. Such sudden popularity led to a building boom and much of the beautiful architecture we associate with the town began to appear at this time. The famous Pantiles, still a magnet today for the aesthetically minded tourist, were laid during this period and the 'olde world' charm of the quaint teashops, gown and antique shops survives even today and stands in sharp contrast to the brash consumerism of the supermarkets that have put in a more recent appearance elsewhere in the town.

The 'Royal' addition to the town's name was granted by King Edward VII in recognition of the popularity the town enjoyed among so many members of the royal family.

Some famous residents (past and present) include Tom Baker (actor), Jo Brand (comedienne), Edward Bulwer-Lytton (writer), Hugh Dowding (RAF officer), Jilly Goolden (TV presenter), David Gower (cricketer), Victor McLaglen (actor), Louise Jameson (actress), Beau Nash (eighteenth-century dandy), William Thackeray (writer) and Virginia Wade (tennis player).

# THE CINQUE PORTS

Some of the ports in Kent had a special role to play not only in the history of the county but in the history of the country as well. From the Middle Ages they were awarded special privileges in return for shouldering much of the burden of defence if the country was attacked. There were originally five ports and they were known collectively as the Cinque Ports (pronounced 'sink ports' and spelled as per the Norman French manner. The modern French for five is *cinq*, and rhymes with 'sank').

The Cinque Ports were formed into a kind of confederation at some time after the Norman Conquest but nobody seems a hundred percent sure of the exact start date. All anybody can be certain about is that at some time during the reign of Henry II (1154–89) what had been a loose association of defensive ports along the south-eastern coast of the country was brought together into a more formal alliance for both commercial and military purposes. The five original towns in the confederation were Romney, Hythe, Dover, Sandwich and Hastings (which was and is in Sussex). As a group they were obliged to provide a total of fifty-seven ships for the Crown's use and each ship was to be manned by a crew of twenty-one (plus one boy) for a total of fifteen days every year. In return for these duties and obligations the Crown granted a number of privileges including:

Freedom from tolls and taxes
Exemption from the jurisdiction of external courts
The right to levy local taxes and administer their own
   courts
The right of 'den and strond' (i.e. they could dry and repair
   their own nets and then organise a Herring Fair as far
   away as the mouth of the River Yare on the coast of
   Norfolk)
The right to appoint representatives to carry the canopy
   over the head of the sovereign at coronations and then
   sit to his or her right at the celebratory banquet.
From 1265 they also had the right to be represented in
   parliament by nominated barons.

By the terms of the 1155 charter they were also granted such weird sounding rights as *soc and sac* (the right to govern themselves), *blodwit and fledwit* (authority to punish anyone who shed blood or attempted to escape justice), *infrangentheof and outfrangentheof* (the right to execute criminals caught inside or outside a port's jurisdiction), *flotsam, jetsam and ligen* (they could keep goods that had been thrown overboard or was just found floating near, or lying on, the shore), *withernam* (the right to take debtors to court and have defaulters punished) and *mundbryce* (the right to inflict punishment on anyone found guilty of a breach of the peace).

The specific taxes and charges from which these ports were exempt included *Lastage*, a tax based on the weight of an item; *Tallage*, tax by the number of items; *Passage*, duty paid when landing goods from ship to shore and *Pontage,* the duty which had to be paid before crossing a bridge.

But the original five towns were not expected to shoulder the considerable expense or fulfil their duties alone. Rye and Winchelsea were added to the list in the thirteenth century as 'antient towns' and then a number of other towns along the south coast were added to lend support (and share the cost). These additional, subsidiary ports were known as 'limbs' and include Tenterden (a limb of Rye), Folkestone (a limb of Dover) and Pevensey (a limb of Hastings). At its peak the confederation boasted a total of forty-two ports and their 'limbs', although not all enjoyed equal status.

The official residence for the Warden of the Cinque Ports was, and still is, Walmer Castle, just outside Deal. Although now mainly of only a ceremonial role, the original five ports have managed to retain their legal status even if their original rights and privileges are seldom, if ever, exercised.

# 7

# LAWLESS KENT

D on't be fooled by Kent's reputation as 'the garden of England'. The picture of rural peace and tranquillity conjured up by such a phrase disguises a multitude of sins and there have been times in the county's history when the men of violence held sway. The orchards and green pastures have seen bloodshed, witnessed rebellion and provided the backdrop to some of the most heinous crimes in the history of England. Rebellion, rioting, mayhem and smuggling have been just a part of Kent's history as have idyllic country pursuits, leisurely pastimes and the quieter occupations of the county's yeomen.

## THE REBELS

*The Peasants' Revolt*
Back in the fourteenth century England had a pretty rough time of it. War, hunger and disease had stalked the land and, for the ordinary folk in particular, life was grim. When Richard II came to the throne as a ten-year-old boy in 1377 the country was experiencing severe financial problems. The Black Death had ravaged the country and the ongoing wars with France proved an ever-present drain on the king's coffers. At the end of the decade French ships raided the south coast and the Isle of Wight, putting great strain on the Cinque Ports which were tasked with the defence of the realm. In a nutshell, more ships were needed to fend off the invader and this meant, inevitably, more taxation to pay for them.

*The First Poll Tax* was levied by the king in 1377. All persons over the age of fifteen were obliged to pay four old pence, known as a groat, to the Crown.

*The Second Poll Tax* was imposed in 1379 but was slightly more equitable as payment depended on status and the ability to pay.

*The Third Poll Tax* was the last straw. In 1380 John of Gaunt, looking after the king's finances, imposed a tax of one shilling on everyone over the age of fifteen. This proved too much and was the spark that set the bonfire of rebellion alight.

The Black Death had been a dreadful tragedy for the country as a whole, but that is not to say that there were not some people who did not benefit from it. The peasantry actually found that they had the whip hand and could make demands on their lords and masters which would have been unthinkable before the plague struck. So many people died in 1348–9 that the country's workforce was seriously depleted and those who survived could pick and choose who to work for and, at the same time and within reason, name their price. In other words, the peasantry had shaken off many of the shackles of feudalism and they saw the introduction of the third poll-tax as a step backward and a threat to enslave them to the lords of the manor yet again.

The seething anger caused by all these extra financial burdens imposed from above just needed someone who could direct it to where it would have some effect. And the man who fitted the bill was **John Ball** (*c.* 1338–81). Known as 'the mad priest of Kent', John Ball was a Lollard, as the followers of John Wycliffe were known. He held very unorthodox religious views (for which at one point he was locked up in Maidstone gaol by the Archbishop of Canterbury) and was also bitterly opposed to the social order of the day. He preached against social injustice and had a particular bee in his bonnet about society being divided into the aristocracy and the peasantry. An early socialist, he spotted that most of the population toiled from dawn until dusk while the idle rich just sat back and enjoyed the fruits of their labours. It was he who came out with the question 'When Adam toiled and Eve span / who was then the gentleman?'

At about the same time there was another hothead in Kent who, when he got wind of the gathering storm of an uprising, could not resist the temptation to get involved. His name was **Walter (aka Wat) Tyler** (though thought to have been born in Essex) and up to the point where he joined the rebellion virtually nothing is known about him. Some sources say that he was an ex-soldier and a bit of a bruiser with a reputation for brawling and getting into trouble. Whatever his past, he answered the call of the times and soon found himself at the head of the rabble marching through Kent to make its demands on the King of England.

For a while the Wat Tyler and John Ball team proved a powerful combination. They were able to lead their peasant army all the way through Kent, gathering strength as they went, finally assembling on Blackheath on 13 June 1381, poised to storm London. And storm it they did. When they reached London the rebels went on the rampage and caused so much mayhem that the king agreed to meet them and discuss their grievances and demands which included:

Abolition of the final remnants of feudalism with peasants becoming free tenants paying four old pence per acre for their land

Poll tax to be abolished

Rebels should be allowed to go home and not be punished for taking part in the uprising

The Church should give up all its property and cease being a rich landowning organisation

There was a brief scuffle during which the Mayor of London struck Wat Tyler with his sword and killed him. Nevertheless, the king appeared to lend a sympathetic ear to the rebels' demands. This had a calming effect on the crowd and slowly but surely they began to disperse and make their way back to their lowly homes in Kent, no doubt somewhat elated at the thought of what they had achieved. But the king went back on his word. Many of the rebels were rounded up and hanged and the promises of ecclesiastical and social reform were conveniently forgotten. John Ball fled, initially to the Weald of Kent, but eventually managed to evade the king's men and make his way to Coventry where he was apprehended. What next awaited him was a cruel fate: he was hanged, drawn and quartered as the young king looked on. Then, to add a final insult to painful injury, his head was taken to London and left on top of a pike on London Bridge as a warning to others. The brief but bitter protest against social injustice was over . . . for the time being.

## Jack Cade's Rebellion

Fast forward now to the year 1450. Between late May and mid-July another rebellion took place in Kent but this time it did not involve the raggle-taggle army of disgruntled peasants. This time the leader was **John (aka Jack) Cade** who claimed to be no less a person than John Mortimer, cousin of the Duke of Kent. His followers were not only the downtrodden tillers of the land but included a knight of the realm, a few squires and soldiers back from the wars in France. But, strangely enough, the demands of this disciplined if irregular army were very similar to those of Tyler and Ball and, almost unbelievably, their fate was virtually a re-run of the historical treachery and chicanery that followed the 1381 rebellion. Among their demands were:

> The abolition of the Statutes of Labourers. These were measures introduced in 1349 and 1351 as the king attempted to deal with the inflationary cycle of higher wages leading to higher prices. The first of the statutes decreed that workers' wages should remain at the pre-Black Death level. The second made it illegal to pay workers higher wages and also for shopkeepers to increase their prices. These measures were both unpopular and almost impossible to enforce.

> The tax system was to be overhauled and abuses on the part of the authorities remedied.

The rebels, like their predecessors, plundered London where they murdered the Lord High Treasurer. They also dragged James

Fiennes (Lord Saye) out of the Tower where he had been placed by King Henry VI and beheaded him. Until he fell out of favour with the king, Lord Saye had been Constable of Dover Castle and, according to Cade and his followers, treated the people of Kent abysmally and taxed them to the hilt.

The situation in London worsened by the hour until eventually the Crown was forced to act. Loyal troops were sent to confront the rebels and, after a long battle, succeeded in restoring calm. Cade and his men were promised a full pardon and redress for their grievances but, just as in 1381, the king went back on his word. As soon as Cade and his army dispersed, the king issued a proclamation annulling his pardon and offering a reward for Cade, dead or alive. The rebel leader was captured, beheaded, and once again London Bridge was adorned with the head of a subject who dared to challenge the king's authority.

Jack Cade was immortalised in Shakespeare's *Henry VI* when Dick, one of Cade's fellow rebels, says 'the first thing we do, let's kill all the lawyers.'

## Wyatt's Rebellion

There were times in the sixteenth century when it was not a good idea to let people know you were a Catholic and there were others when, if you were Protestant, you kept quiet about it. Queen Mary, the daughter of Henry VIII and his Spanish first wife, Catherine of Aragón, was never reconciled to her father's break with Rome and hid her adherence to Catholicism from no-one. When she then contemplated marrying the Catholic Philip of Spain, Protestants slept badly at night and feared that the whole country was about to revert to Catholicism. Some, including Sir Thomas Wyatt the Younger, the wealthy and influential landowner down in Kent, wanted to see Elizabeth on the throne and to secure England's future as a country free from the shackles of Rome.

Other Protestant men of some standing in the land joined Wyatt in his determination to do something about the situation. Sir James Croft, a Herefordshire landowner, Sir Peter Crew of Devon and Henry Grey, 1st Duke of Suffolk all joined in the conspiracy. The plan was that each should lead an uprising in his part of the country and then converge on London. They would then depose Mary and place her half-sister Elizabeth on the throne. Right from the start the plan seemed doomed to failure. The only one of the conspirators who managed to raise anything like an adequate force to finish the job was Wyatt who, on 26 January, occupied Rochester and proclaimed his intentions to depose Mary. It appears that there were a good many people of like mind and he was able to muster together 3,000 men. This number was promptly swelled when a band of 1,000 militiamen was dispatched from London to quell what was now seen as open rebellion but immediately changed sides. All seemed to be going well for Wyatt and his followers as they headed for London but when they reached Southwark they met stiff opposition. Mary had herself delivered a rousing speech and had put some backbone into the city's defenders who saw off the rebels with not too much difficulty. Refusing to recognise defeat, the rebels altered course a little and marched on Ludgate, but here they were stopped in their tracks and their army crushed. The rebellion was over and Mary safe on her throne.

Sir Thomas Wyatt, along with a further ninety rebels, was tried and executed. His family went through the agony of being stripped of all their titles and having all their lands confiscated. They were only restored to them after Elizabeth ascended the throne in 1558.

# THE RIOTERS

## *The Plum Pudding Riots*

The Puritans were a dour lot. They did not like the thought of people actually enjoying themselves and at the same time considered much of organised religion little more than superstition. For the Puritans church services had to be modest, understated affairs with absolutely no element that could by any stretch of the imagination be associated with idolatry. They also believed that important dates in the religious calendar should be 'fast' days as opposed to 'feast' days and so it seemed to them that Christmas should be banned. But when they tried to abolish seasonal festivities in Canterbury in 1647 they soon found that the people of the city had other ideas.

The task of conveying to the people the news that the government had cancelled Christmas fell to the mayor, William Bridge, and he announced that:

> No plum pottage (pudding) or festive pies were to be made. Oliver Cromwell himself is reported as saying that anything as delicious as mince pies had to be the work of the devil.

> All shops were to remain open on 25 December and trade was to be conducted as normal.

> No holly or other 'superstitious herb' was to be used to decorate homes or adorn doorways.

> No church services were to be held on 25 December. (Incidentally, if Christmas Day had fallen on a Sunday there would have been no problem and church services could have been held as normal. But in 1647 Christmas Day fell on a Wednesday (Gregorian calendar) or Saturday (Julian calendar) so any services would have been a special religious ceremony. This is what was so unacceptable to the Puritans.)

Acceptance of these orders from above was less than enthusiastic. In fact the populace rioted as they wanted their traditional Christmas with a church service in the morning and then no doubt some good old-fashioned gluttony, merriment and liquid refreshment for the rest of the day. The mayor did his best to quell the crowd's anger and persuade them to obey the laws of the land, but to no avail. He ended up in the gutter although he did manage to pick himself up and lose himself in the mêlée. The following day he shot one of the crowd during a further disturbance and this time had to flee for his life to avoid the wrath of the baying mob. He disappeared for a few weeks and the mob took control of the city, went on the rampage and caused a fair amount of damage. Not until the end of January did a force of some 3,000 Parliamentarian soldiers smash down the city gates and part of the walls before storming the city and recapturing it from the mob. The rather unusual Christmas 'celebrations' of 1647 were finally over.

## The Swing Riots

This is something of a misnomer. The Swing riots, by and large, did not involve angry crowds venting their ire on the forces of law and order or pitched battles between disgruntled citizens and soldiers of the Crown. The title refers more to a period of a couple of years during which acts of what we now refer to as terrorism gave many a landowner or magistrate in Kent sleepless nights, particularly if they were unfortunate enough to receive one of the dreaded letters signed 'Captain Swing'.

But 'Captain Swing' did not exist. The signature was nothing more than a collective pseudonym designed to protect the identity of the person or persons who sent the letter. And the letter was always a threat that the recipient was on the list of targets for the nocturnal activities of a band of farm labourers who had reached the end of their tether. These were, for the most part, ordinary working folk with families to keep who saw no way of hitting back at the system other than burning hayricks and destroying farm machinery, in particular the threshing machines.

The campaign of terror began in 1830 after a succession of disastrous harvests and extremely hard winters during which the people at the bottom of the rural social ladder suffered almost beyond endurance. Their wages were barely enough to keep body and soul together and there was precious little hope of any improvement. The end of the wars with France meant that hundreds of ex-soldiers came home and, needing to find work, sought employment on the farms and estates in Kent. At the same time advances in agricultural technology meant that machinery could often do the work of perhaps a dozen men in half the time and these two factors coincided to make the outlook very bleak for rural workers. A landowner could hire those who would work for least and if he bought himself a piece of the new-fangled technology he could reduce his workforce to a minimum. In other words the rural labourer was caught by the nineteenth century version of a 'double whammy'.

But there were other factors that contributed to the terrible plight of the country folk:

The end of the so-called 'living-in' system. It had been the custom for centuries for farm workers to live on the farm almost as members of the farmer's family. In the early nineteenth century this system began to die out and a labourer had to find his own place to live. Furthermore, he was now treated as a hired hand and was paid when there was work but not when there was none.

The government's attitude to the poor became increasingly unsympathetic. It became fashionable to see Poor Law relief as encouraging idleness and so the amount a starving labourer could claim was cut. The rural crime rate soared and poaching in particular became a serious problem.

Church tithes. These had originally been paid in the form of one-tenth of a parish harvest going to the local church authorities. Later on the grain, etc. was replaced by a cash payment by landowners and workers alike to pay the parson's wages. The landowners could usually afford it, but for the cash-strapped labourer it was simply beyond the meagre contents of his purse.

By 1831 the 'Swing Riots' in Kent had begun to peter out. Some rioters were hanged and many were deported, although it has to be said also that the majority were simply pardoned by JPs who were not unsympathetic to their cause. The riots might have contributed to the 1834 Poor Law Amendment Act, but this is not certain. All that is certain is that, despite their minor revolution, the agricultural labourers of Kent saw little if any improvement in the living conditions.

## THE SMUGGLERS

Kent is a perfect place for smugglers. It lies just a few miles from France and its own gently sloping beaches make landing and dragging contraband goods ashore a relatively easy task. In the eighteenth century, when smuggling was at its height, many a beach near Deal, Folkestone and Hythe echoed to the crunching sound of the 'free-traders' (as they liked to think of themselves), hauling the 'brandy for the parson, baccy for the clerk' over the shingle before loading it on to packhorses to be spirited (no pun intended!) off the beach and sent on its way to London. It was a swashbuckling time when daring young men ran rings around the Excise Men (well, most of the time) as they conducted their parallel import/export business in an effort to satisfy what was an eager clientele and a ready market. The government tried to stamp out the trade but too many 'respectable' members of society were complicit in it for attempts at curbing it to have much chance of success.

The causes of smuggling are not hard to assess and can probably be traced back to just one word: taxation. The government of the day was short of money, in no small measure because of the endless wars this country seemed to be involved in right up to the demise of Napoleon in 1815. Spirits, tobacco, linen and tea were taxed so heavily that, if he was not caught in the act, a smuggler could make a handsome living from his chosen trade. He could sail over to France, buy (as opposed to steal) whatever his chosen wares were for the trip, come home and sell them for far less than the going rate on this side of the Channel, thus making a very handsome profit.

In the very early days of smuggling, in the seventeenth century, however, the trade was rather different. In the first place, the commodity involved was mainly wool and the direction was the other way round: smugglers took their contraband out of England and smuggled it into France. (The verb 'to smuggle' entered English from German and Dutch around the 1660s meaning 'to transport illegally'. It comes from and old Scandinavian root meaning 'to creep into a hole' or 'to conceal oneself' and so has obvious applications to any activity involving crawling into caves and wishing to remain unobserved.)

The trade in wool smuggling expanded enormously in the seventeenth century because:

> the wool trade of the Weald of Kent had largely collapsed and thus workers and traders associated with the industry found themselves unemployed.

> the importance of the Cinque Ports declined and they were deprived of their special tax exemptions.

there were thousands of sheep grazing on the luscious
pastures of Romney Marsh.

there was a ready market in France for good quality English
wool.

In 1614 the export of English wool was declared illegal and
in 1661 it was made punishable by death.

Smuggling into France is thought to have started in about
1300 during the reign of Edward I after duty had been put on
wool, a commodity in plentiful supply in Kent and for which
there was a thriving market on the Continent. At first the tax was
minimal and those who attempted to evade paying it were few,
but when it was made illegal to export wool (the government's
attempt at protecting the weaving trade) and then later on
when it was declared a crime punishable by death there was,
paradoxically, an increase rather than a decrease in smuggling.
And those involved armed themselves to the teeth as it now
became even more important to avoid capture by the king's men.
By the 1670s the trade had taken on a far more professional look.
Instead of a few disorganised bands of amateurs plying to and
fro across the Channel, the 'big boys' moved in and applied their
not inconsiderable entrepreneurial skills. The little boats were
replaced with bigger, faster and better armed ships to ferry the
contraband out of England across to France.

For a while the 'free-traders' carried on their illicit enterprise
with not too much trouble from the authorities. When the threat
to their activities did come it came from the French side of the
operation: the customers on the other side of the Channel found
out that they could get wool of equal quality from Ireland for the
same price and with less interference from the Customs officials.
Now the original 'owlers', as the smugglers were known because
of the nocturnal shenanigans, spread their wings a little and
looked for additional and/or alternative commodities with which
to fill their boats: they decided that the reduced exports of wool
could be offset by importing brandy, tobacco, silks and tea. And
tea, at one point, was by far the most profitable commodity for the
smugglers. There was a heavy tax on the leaf in England (by 1784

it had reached 119 per cent) but virtually none in the countries of Europe and this made it an obvious target for the profit-obsessed gangs. It has been estimated that by the late eighteenth century two-thirds of all tea consumed in the homes and coffee houses of England had been smuggled in past the coast guards. Intrerestingly tea was originally sold in England in coffee houses and the first tea shop did not make its appearance until 1864. The first tea room was opened by Thomas Twining in 1706 at 216 The Strand, London, and is still there today.

It was about this time also that organised crime in the shape of smugglers' gangs began to appear. Officials were bribed (by all accounts without too much persuading) and it was not unknown for large sections of communities close to the coast to be involved in some capacity in the now flourishing trade. But it would be a mistake to believe that all the smugglers had to do was drop a little bribe here and there to have the honest citizens queueing up to help. Many were willing, but if the smugglers came across the resistance of high-minded citizens they were by no means hesitant in applying serious pressure: physical beatings, blackmail, extortion and even murder were all weapons in the armoury which they were quite willing to use to coerce people into helping them in their nefarious deeds. In fact, it was the speed with which some members of these violent gangs resorted to non-verbal means of persuasion that led to their eventual downfall.

## THE SMUGGLER GANGS

### *The Hawkhurst Gang*

Operating between 1735 and 1749, the Hawkhurst gang was probably the largest of the smuggler bands that plagued the south-east in the eighteenth and nineteenth centuries. With something in the region of 500 members they operated out of the village of Hawkhurst which lies about 10 miles to the north of Romney Marsh. Any notions of the romantic smuggler just out to earn enough to feed his wife and kids can be discounted with this lot. On the contrary, they were able to amass personal fortunes which must have been the envy of many a law-abiding citizen who earned his crust by more socially acceptable means. The smugglers were cut-throats who terrorised the local communities as well as frightening the life out of all but the most determined Revenue (or Excise) officers. The gang members thought nothing of seriously injuring any of the king's men who got in their way and they had one particularly nasty way of dealing with them: they would give them a thrashing to within an inch of their lives and then dump them on the French coast. As Britain was at war with France at this time we can only imagine the fate that awaited many of those picked up on the other side of the Channel.

When trade was a bit slack and the gang members had nothing else to do they would indulge in a little highway robbery or make a thorough nuisance of themselves among the villagers. Their favourite meeting place (and unofficial headquarters) was the **Oak and Ivy Inn** in the village and no doubt their drunken antics made them very unpopular with the locals. But they also frequented the **Star and Eagle Inn** in Goudhurst and it was here that they met their undoing. In April 1747 soldiers of the king were sent to confront the gang and, after a bitter fight, thoroughly routed them. The leaders, Arthur Gray and Thomas Kingsmill, were hanged in 1748 and 1749 respectively.

## The North Kent Gang

As the name suggests, this gang of smugglers operated on the north coast of Kent around places such as Chalk (near Gravesend), Reculver and Ramsgate. During the 1780s they would bring their contraband ashore near Reculver and then stash it away in the caves near Margate. At first they seem to have confined themselves to simply smuggling goods into England to make what they saw as an honest living. But by 1820 they began resorting to violence and at one point managed to release some of their most violent members from Faversham gaol. They murdered a certain Midshipman Snow in 1821 and some of them were tried at the Old Bailey but acquitted; it has been suggested that the acquittal was due to the jury being sympathetic to the smugglers' calling. Some time later, however, the same gang was caught in a violent exchange with officers of the law in Westgate-on-Sea near Margate and eighteen of them arrested. Four were hanged and the rest of the gang were sentenced to be transported to Van Diemen's Land (later named Tasmania) for life.

## The Groombridge Gang

Geographically Groombridge straddles the border between Kent and East Sussex, but as the gang's activities were carried out mainly on Romney Marsh it can justifiably be included in an inventory of Kent's smugglers.

The gang began operation in the 1730s under the leadership of John Bowra, but after his arrest by the authorities in 1737 leadership passed to Robert Moreton. Both Bowra and Moreton organised sophisticated distribution networks for their contraband (especially tea) so that there was a near constant supply of their valuable commodity to their clients in London. Bowra was born in 1713 into a reasonably well-to-do family and it is known that he was, by profession, a land surveyor. His father was a churchwarden and his grandfather had practised as a surgeon in Sevenoaks. Robert Moreton's background is far less well known. In fact all we seem to know about him is that he rode with the Hawkhurst gang as well as the Groombridge boys, and was 'grassed' by an informer in 1749. Possibly the informer was a member of the gang, or (more probably) a member of the public, fed up to the back teeth with being terrorised by what he considered to be just a band of cut-throats.

## The Aldington Gang

A bit of a late-comer to the smuggling game, the Aldington gang took its name from the village just south of Ashford where it had the local inn, the Walnut Tree, as its headquarters. Its leader was a farmer, George Ransley, who obviously liked to top up his agricultural income with a bit of 'free trade' on the side. But his entrepreneurial skills did not stop there: he kept back a certain amount of the smuggled spirits and sold it quite openly from his own cottage. In fact, he was so open about his little cottage industry that his establishment was known locally as 'the Bourne Tap'.

Unfortunately, like so many of their ilk, the gang started to bully the locals and indulge in more and more anti-social, criminal activities and so lost both the active and tacit support of the villagers. They were eventually arrested and many of the gang members were shipped off to Van Diemen's Land, never to return.

*Sign outside a pub in Aldington with strong smuggling connections.*

## SMUGGLERS' PUBS IN KENT

| | |
|---|---|
| Gravesend | The Three Dawes |
| Isle of Grain | The Hogarth Inn |
| Conyer | The Ship Inn |
| Seasalter | The Blue Anchor Inn |
| Whitstable | The Old Neptune |
| Herne Bay | The Ship Inn |
| | The Smugglers' Inn |
| Broadstairs (St Peter's) | The Fig Tree Inn |
| Pegwell | The Belle View Tavern |

| | |
|---|---|
| Deal | The Ship and Smuggler |
| Grafty Green (Maidstone) | The King's Head |
| Wrotham | The Vigo Inn |
| Lydd | The Pilot Inn |
| Ivychurch | The Bell |
| Dymchurch | The Ship Hotel |
| Hythe | The Red Lion |
| | The Bell |
| | The Smuggler's Retreat |
| Aldington | The Walnut Tree |
| Woodchurch | The Six Bells |
| | The Bonny Cravat |
| Hawkhurst | The Oak and Ivy Inn |
| Sissinghurst | The Bull Inn |
| Goudhurst | The Star and Eagle Inn |
| Groombridge | The Crown Inn |

# SOME FAMOUS NAMES FROM THE SMUGGLING WORLD

**Slippery Sam.** The nickname of Samuel Johnson, who was born in Kent in 1730. As the son of a smuggler he followed in his father's footsteps and, as soon as he was able, bought a farmhouse near the village of Petham, a mile or two south of Canterbury. He used the building to store contraband which had been brought in from the Continent. He also devised a plan of weighting his smuggled goods and hiding them on the bottom of a nearby pond. His lucrative career came to a sudden end in about 1760 when he was arrested, tried and hanged.

**Richard Joy.** A man of enormous size and supposedly weighing 25 stone he was caught smuggling red-handed and forced to 'volunteer' to serve in His Majesty's Navy. He was a native of Broadstairs and, on release from the navy, returned there and resumed his former occupation. He does not appear to have been a particularly successful smuggler as he was caught in the act again, but this time he drowned as he was attempting to escape. He was only thirty-seven years old.

**Joss Snelling.** Another Broadstairs free-trader, he was involved in the famous skirmish with the Excise men at Botany Bay (the one near Broadstairs, Kent, not the one in Australia) in 1769 when Snelling shot one of his pursuers. His fate was one of the most fortunate among his smuggling colleagues; he lived to the ripe old age of ninety-six.

## DAYS OF SYN

Every two years the good people of Dymchurch hold a pageant known as a 'Day of Syn' when the novels of Russell Thorndike are brought to life. The first was held in 1964 when the then vicar dreamed up the idea as a means of raising money for the church roof. The first year was so successful that it has become a tradition to hold the pageant biennially and it now attracts visitors from as far afield as Australia and the United States.

# 8

# DEFENCE OF
# THE REALM

Kent has often been referred to as 'front-line Kent' and not without justification. Several would-be invaders from the Continent have taken advantage of the shortest sea crossing to these islands and, with varying degrees of success, attempted to gain a foothold on Kent's largely undefended coastal areas. The Romans eventually managed it, William the Conqueror landed in the neighbouring county of Sussex, and others tried but never enjoyed the success of their predecessors. After 1066 it was another 522 years before anyone else made a serious attempt. This time it was Spain who decided to send her fleet against England.

## 1588 – THE SPANISH ARMADA

As news filtered through that Spain, one of the most powerful nations in Europe at the time, was preparing to invade England, the people of Kent must have been worried. They were only too aware that if an invasion was coming there was a good chance it would be the inhabitants of places such as Dover, Deal, Folkestone and Hythe that would have a vital role to play in repelling the enemy. Fortunately, they escaped being put to the test . . . but only just.

### The causes
Mary, Queen of England, was married to Philip of Spain, and so the country was in effect Catholic. When Mary died the next in line to the throne was Mary, Queen of Scots, but she had been

*A replica of a beacon typical of those erected all along the south coast, from Cornwall to Kent, to warn of the approach of the Spanish Armada.*

executed by Elizabeth after what many saw as her illegal accession to the Crown. Philip, despite the fact that he had returned to Spain and had effectually abandoned his wife, viewed Elizabeth as a usurper who had seized the Crown of England in an effort to further the Protestant cause.

The Pope (Sixtus V) viewed England's return to Protestantism with horror. He therefore supported Philip in what they both regarded as a crusade.

England had supported the Dutch rebels who wanted independence from Spain as the Netherlands had long been ruled by the Spanish. Philip saw an invasion of England as an opportunity for revenge.

A successful invasion of England would be a way of putting an end to Francis Drake's pillaging of Spanish vessels in and around the Caribbean Sea.

England was isolated within Europe and seen as relatively weak by Spain.

## Singeing the King of Spain's Beard

A year before the Armada made its appearance in the Channel, Sir Francis Drake had sailed into Cádiz Bay and set fire to many of the warships lying at anchor. The affair came to be known as 'singeing the King of Spain's beard' and was yet another reason why the Spanish were not too enamoured of the English.

## The ships

England has always been a maritime country, but in the sixteenth century (which Spaniards refer to as their *siglo de oro* 'Golden Century') Spain was also a powerful seagoing nation. Like England, she had conquered territories all over the known world and was forging ahead with the discovery of new lands beyond

*An English ship typical of those sent out to meet the threat from the Armada.*

the horizon. Consequently, her knowledge and skill in navigation, seamanship and shipbuilding were at least equal to those of any other nation. The ships Spain launched against England in 1588 included:

*The Galleon.* At the time this was the Leviathan of the high seas. It was the battleship of most sixteenth-century European navies, even though we always tend to think in terms of 'Spanish' galleons. Usually these ships consisted of several decks and were armed typically with thirty demi-culverin cannon capable of firing shot weighing 8–10 lbs, with an effective range of about 1,800ft. In 1588 the Armada which sailed against England included twenty-two galleons.

*Galleys* and *galleasses.* These were ships that had changed very little in design since Roman times. They were large and powered by a combination of sail and oars. The Armada had four of each of these ships and are an indicator of Spanish naval tactics: galleys and galleasses were designed for ramming enemy vessels below the water line.

*Converted merchant ships.* These were intended mainly for the transport of troops. The initial complement of 18,000 soldiers was to be supplemented by troops from the Netherlands before the invasion of England began.

## The plan

Philip II and his military planners devised a plan which should have worked. At the end of May the Armada (which the Spaniards referred to as *la Grande y Felicísima Armada* 'the Great and Most Fortunate Navy') sailed from Portugal (at the time occupied by Spain) and set a course for England under the command of the Duke of Medina Sedonia. According to the plans he was to pick up an invasion force in the region of Calais, invade the Kent coast, landing around Margate, and then head straight for London where he was to capture the queen. But things did not go according to plan.

## Intelligence

We have all heard the stories of how Sir Francis Drake nonchalantly claimed that he had plenty of time to finish his game of bowls and then chase 'the Dons' all the way back to Spain. The truth, however, is somewhat different. Drake did not give the Armada a thrashing off the coast of Devon; in fact, his ships hardly made contact with the enemy. Drake knew that he was almost certainly outgunned by the Spanish galleons and all he was able to do was follow them as they made steady progress up through the English Channel as far as Calais. And this is where the importance of military intelligence came into play.

Sir Francis Drake captured a Spanish vessel, *El Rosario,* soon after it entered the English Channel and this provided the English with some very valuable intelligence about their adversary. The gun-decks on Spanish men-o'-war were so cramped for space that there was virtually no room for the Spanish gunners to manoeuvre the cannon and reload. This led Drake to the conclusion that the major Armada tactic was for the crew to fire a single salvo and then prepare to ram and board enemy ships.

On English ships there was plenty of space for the gunners to fire and reload and so Vice-Admiral Drake and Admiral Howard realised that all they had to do was make sure they had enough powder and shot to keep reloading and thus keep the Spanish at bay and deprive them of the chance to board the English ships. In brief, the English made sure they deprived the Spanish of an opportunity to put their strengths to good use at the same time as making sure they had every opportunity of maximising their own.

## The big mistakes

Nobody underestimated the might of the Spanish Armada. Its reputation had gone before it throughout the known world and, had it not been for a number of miscalculations, it could probably have defeated the English and subjected England to Spanish rule for goodness knows how long.

The first mistakes concerned basic planning. The man originally in charge of the Armada was the very able Álvaro de Bazán.

He was a navy man through and through with salt water in his veins but he unfortunately (for Spain, not for England!) died a few months before the Armada was due to sail. Unbelievably, Philip replaced him with a wealthy, landlubber aristocrat, Alonso Pérez de Guzmán, the Duke of Medina Sidonia, who was a capable soldier and commander of land armies but had limited knowledge of sailing or the conduct of naval warfare. Recent archaeological evidence has come to light that serious mistakes were made concerning the ships and materiel chosen for the invasion, including the fact that Spanish galleons were top heavy, making them vulnerable in strong winds. In the case of the support ships, many were suited more to the Mediterranean than the rough English Channel and North Sea. Furthermore, the gunpowder used by the Spaniards was of inferior manufacture and the cannonballs could be less than effective. The way in which they were manufactured made them brittle with a tendency to shatter on impact, causing little damage to the hulls of English ships. By contrast, English cannonballs seldom failed to penetrate the Spanish hulls sending deadly showers of splinters and shards of metal, which acted like modern shrapnel, across the gun-decks. Then there was the question of victuals: the Armada set sail in May and did not reach the Channel until mid-July by which time much of the food was rotten and the water undrinkable. The result was that by the time the Armada reached its destination disease, hunger and thirst had almost sapped the Spaniards of their ability to fight.

Equally serious was the lack of military preparation. Medina Sidonia had neglected what should have been a major consideration during the planning stage of the whole undertaking: there was no deepwater harbour on the coast of Flanders where he was supposed to pick up the main body of his invasion force. Consequently the Armada was forced to lie at anchor outside Calais harbour and this meant that it was vulnerable.

Probably the most important failure, however, in the planning of the operation was the over-reliance on communications. Difficult at the best of times, once the Armada had set sail communications between the King in Madrid, Medina Sidonia with the Armada at sea and the Duke of Alba in the Netherlands must have been so slow as to be almost worthless. The result was that the right hand seldom knew what the left was doing and consequently the complex planning just fell apart. When Medina Sidonia finally arrived at what was supposed to be the rendezvous point the invasion army was not there and, even if it had been, communications had been so bad that no suitable barges had been provided to transfer the soldiers onto the waiting ships.

## The final blow

While the Armada was making good speed with a following wind the ships maintained a crescent formation which meant that they were almost totally impervious to attack. But as soon as the ships dropped anchor, as they did at Calais on 27 July, they presented a sitting-duck target to the English. During the night Drake and his men sent fire-ships into the Armada's midst and caused havoc among the Spanish sailors. The last thing on earth that they wanted was eight blazing ships around them which could set fire to their own vessels, heavily laden as they were with gunpowder; the consequences of such an encounter were just too awful to even contemplate. So they set about frantically slicing through anchor cables and scattering as fast as possible as they struggled to put the maximum distance between themselves and the fire-ships. None of the Armada ships was lost at this point, but several were destroyed during the Battle of Gravelines the following day. The battle proved to be inconclusive as both sides were running seriously short of ammunition, but Medina Sidonia must have realised that this was the beginning of the end; he attempted to hold his position for a while but was eventually forced to join those of his ships which had already set a northerly course. The once 'Invincible Armada' now headed up the eastern coast of England, pursued for a time by Howard, Drake and the English fleet. No contact was made during the chase and eventually the English turned back, leaving Medina Sidonia and his men to the mercy of what turned out to be some of the most violent storms the North Sea had seen for a generation. What Howard, Drake and the other English sailors had failed to do the elements now achieved. The English navy, realistically, had done little more than dent the might of the Armada but the storms caused such havoc that by the time it had sailed around the north of Scotland, down the western coast of Ireland and limped home to Spain, barely 50 per cent of the original complement of ships remained. King Philip, distraught on hearing the fate of Spain's pride and joy, could only comment 'I sent the Armada against men, not against God's winds and waves.'

Perhaps so, but the people of Kent still breathed a sigh of relief.

## 1803–5 – THE THREAT OF NAPOLEON

This was the next occasion when the people of Kent had something to worry about. Since the French Revolution and the advent of Napoleon people throughout Britain had lived in the shadow of either bloody anti-monarchist uprisings inspired by the events on the other side of the Channel, or a direct invasion by France's *L Armée d'Angleterre* (Army for England). Looking back on those times the concerns men had about what the future held might seem like paranoia, but in the early years of the nineteenth century the inhabitants of places such as Kent, Sussex and almost the whole of the south coast, had good reason to be alarmed. All the evidence seemed to suggest that 'Boney' was getting ready to complete his conquest of Europe by crushing little England. France and England declared war on each other in 1803 and it was no secret that Napoleon, who had destroyed some of the finest armies in Europe, had turned his gaze towards the all-too-tempting prize of the little offshore island. He himself stated at one point that he wanted to plant the Imperial Eagle on the Tower of London and if he could just rid the Channel of English men-o'-war for six hours, he would be able to rule the world. In fact, his confidence was running so high that he erected a monument in Boulogne commemorating his magnificent victory before he had even set sail.

### The defence
After declaring war and taking account of Napoleon's past successes in Europe, William Pitt (the Younger) and his government came up with the following measures for the protection of the country:

The construction of a chain of defensive forts known as Martello Towers along the Kent coast.

The digging of a canal to slow down the invading French force if it decided to land and then move inland across Romney Marsh.

Preparations for the removal of the government from London to somewhere in the Midlands.

The installation of a new semaphore/telegraph signalling system to improve communications.

Arrangements for the possible evacuation of the population of Kent further inland.

## The Martello Towers
These circular, squat-looking forts take their name from the distorted form of Cape Mortella on the island of Corsica, where the prototype had been encountered by British troops who were impressed by the fort's ability to withstand an attack. When the

*A Martello Tower between Hythe and Dymchurch.*

invasion seemed imminent the government of the day ordered a series of them to be built along the south coast of Kent and Sussex. The hope was that, should the Frenchies decide to invade, the Martello Towers would prove to be a formidable obstacle to any army that dared to set foot on an English beach.

Considering the urgency of the times, it is a little odd that construction work on these towers did not commence until 1805 when the threat of invasion had actually passed. Nevertheless, between 1805 and 1808 a total of seventy-four were constructed between Folkestone and Seaford in Sussex (a distance of just under 63 miles). Normally each fort was about 30ft high with walls 13ft thick on the seaward side. They would house a detachment of about twenty men plus one officer who, in the event of attack, would defend the surrounding area with musket fire and the one cannon mounted on the roof. In two places, Dymchurch in Kent and Eastbourne in Sussex, there were special forts known as 'grand redoubts'. These were massive constructions manned by up to 350 men and armed with eleven cannon and, had they been used, would no doubt have been capable of inflicting serious casualties on an enemy.

In Kent about twenty-five of these buildings survive. Some have been preserved as museums, some have been left to fall into neglect and some have been converted into interesting if somewhat unusual private houses.

## The Royal Military Canal

One of the not-so-bright ideas that someone came up with for defending Kent was to flood Romney Marsh. This idea was soon abandoned as, presumably, it dawned on the military planners that such a move would simply move the landing place for the invading French a few miles inland. The next idea was to construct a water barrier, eventually known as the Royal Military Canal, which in effect cut off the whole of Romney Marsh from the rest of the county. The idea sounds fine, but there were those among the planners who expressed the opinion that a canal was hardly likely to prove much of an obstacle to a determined army. Did those who proposed the idea really believe that this narrow stretch of water would stop the most powerful army in Europe? Had not Napoleon's soldiers coped with far more daunting obstacles as they fought their way across some of the most difficult terrain and fast-flowing rivers in Austria and modern Germany? Was this not the army, after all, that had crossed the Alps in 1800 before crushing the Austrians at Marengo? Were the soldiers of *L'Armée d'Angleterre* really going to come unstuck and lay down their arms when they came face to face with . . . a canal? Perhaps it is just as well that 'Mr Pitt's Ditch', as it was disparagingly referred to at the time, was never put to the test.

Nevertheless, despite the misgivings of some, plans went ahead and work began on the project in October 1804 and was completed in 1809 or 1810 (different sources give different dates). It stretches for 28 miles from a point near Folkestone to Hastings in Sussex and is 30ft wide.

The Royal Military Canal still exists today, although its function has changed somewhat. It is now mainly a tourist attraction where visitors can enjoy a leisurely stroll along its banks or hire a boat for a pleasurable half-hour sailing at will up and down the canal's ever calm and placid waters. Only the occasional models of nineteenth-century soldiers, encountered here and there on the banks, remind visitors of its original role as part of Albion's defences.

---

# HARK!

All Men of stout Heart and Patriotic nature!

## FOLKESTONE VOLUNTEER ARTILLERY

Requires recruits to swell its ranks to prevent the Upstart Napoleon and his French hordes from invading these shores.

If you suffer a Severe Master, a Cruel Landlord or a nagging wife, then accept the King's Shilling and be recruited into the Artillery that is renowned for its Bravery, its Discipline and its Manly bearing, both on and off the field of battle.

Wear the Blue coat of a British Gunner and be admired by the ladies and feared by the French!

Any man of good appearance and intelligence, provided he suffers no missing fingers, lameness nor the pox will be welcome to Enlist in this Fine Company!

God save the King!

---

*A recruitment poster of the times.*

## Napoleon's invasion plans

Before he got down to some serious planning Napoleon considered a couple of astoundingly impractical ideas:

A Channel tunnel! The idea was first suggested to Napoleon in 1802 when Britain and France were (albeit briefly) not at war with each other. The mining engineer Albert Mathieu convinced

*A statue of a soldier on the canal bank at Hythe.*

Napoleon of the feasibility of the project and then, when war resumed in 1803, the military possibilities of a tunnel beneath the English Channel had to be worth at least some consideration. Only when the technical problems and astronomical cost became clear was the idea abandoned.

Flying his troops across the Channel in balloons. The first successful Channel crossing by balloon had been in 1785 and there had been an organisation in existence since 1794 known as the *Compagnie d'Aérostatiers* (Company of Balloonists) which was concerned with the possible military uses of balloons. (Technically speaking, this organisation can claim to be the world's first air force.) Napoleon was advised that the plan was impracticable because of the impossibility of predicting the wind direction.

It might also have dawned on him that a company of reasonably skilled musketeers on the ground could inflict terrible damage on troop-carrying balloons hovering almost motionless above the English coastline.

When he put aside these childish fantasies, Napoleon did come up with what could have been a good plan. He knew that, whereas he was virtually invincible on land, the Royal Navy under Nelson was equally formidable at sea. He realised that if he was to have any hope at all of getting his army across the Channel he would have to neutralise England's warships. Defeating them in open battle was highly improbable and so he devised a plan to draw Nelson's ships away from *La Manche* and thus make sure that, when his invasion fleet left Boulogne, there would be fewer of *les rosbifs* around to destroy his men-o'-war.

At the beginning of hostilities Nelson had blockaded most of the European ports from Toulon in the south of France to Texel in Holland and effectively bottled up the French fleet. Napoleon now ordered Admiral Villeneuve, based in Toulon, to break out, link up with the Spanish fleet at Cádiz and set sail for the Americas. Once in the West Indies they were to join forces with a battle squadron which had already evaded the blockade at Rochefort and begin attacking British interests.

The assumption was that Nelson, once he heard of British colonies being attacked, would set a course for the West Indies and engage the French navy. At this point, Villeneuve would head back across the Atlantic, make contact with the battle squadron from Brest, and invade the south coast of England. Hopefully, while *L'Armée d'Angleterre* was raping and pillaging in Kent, Nelson would either still be chasing ghosts in the West Indies or languishing somewhere in mid-Atlantic. But the plan, which sounded fine on paper, failed because:

Villeneuve failed to link up with the Brest fleet.

Nelson realised what was happening and sent a fast brig back to England to warn the government.

He also made it back to European waters in time to intercept any invasion fleet between Boulogne and the Kent coast.

Meanwhile, Napoleon had assembled a huge invasion army in and around Boulogne and issued orders for the troops to train, prepare for and rehearse the invasion. In August 1804 a full rehearsal was ordered and Napoleon himself supervised arrangements. But the 'dummy run' ended in utter failure, if not total disaster. The choppy seas overturned many of the landing craft, some larger craft either sank or were severely damaged and hundreds of men drowned.

The invasion of England was cancelled, *L'Armée d'Angleterre* was disbanded and transformed into *La Grande Armée*. And the 'Great Army' was ordered to turn around and march eastwards. Once again the people of England and Kent could relax a little and indulge in a peaceful slumber free of the threat of invasion. But a hundred and thirty-odd years later they had a rude awakening.

## THE SECOND WORLD WAR

Everyone knew that war was just over the horizon. Throughout most of the 1930s Hitler left nobody in any doubt that he had plans for the expansion of Germany and was more than prepared to use force to achieve his aims. The rise of Fascism, the Spanish Civil War, the bombing of Guernica (1937), the annexation of Austria and the Sudetenland (1938) all pointed to just one outcome. Then, in September 1939 when Hitler's troops poured over the border into Poland, all lingering doubts were removed and last-minute hopes dashed; Britain and Germany were on a collision course. Chamberlain's announcement to the nation on 3 September that war had been declared took nobody by surprise.

*How they got it a bit wrong . . .*

'My Luftwaffe is invincible . . . And so now we turn to England. How long will this one last – two, three weeks?' *Hermann Goering, Chief of the Luftwaffe, June 1940*

'How long would they last in battle? They ran away from Dunkirk; they deserted France completely for the safety of home. England is there to be taken'. *Hugo Sperrle, Luftwaffe General, June 1940*

The threat of invasion was again very real, and once again it looked as though the invading troops would land in Kent. But the new threat had a vital ingredient that was lacking in previous wars: aeroplanes. And in 1939 both sides knew that the first thing Hitler would have to do was to destroy Britain's air defences if the invasion was to have a chance of success. So as soon as his armies had reached the French Channel ports Hitler, together with Goering, began planning the total destruction of the Royal Air Force. And among their first targets was shipping in the English Channel. The reason for this was quite simple: the Luftwaffe commanders reasoned that if they could lure RAF fighters and interceptors from their bases to defend the ships they could then be attacked and destroyed. The plan did not work because Air Marshal Dowding realised what the Germans were up to and held his fighters back for the more important battle to come. He was criticised severely for leaving the ships to fend for themselves, but his determination to stick to his guns (literally and metaphorically) paid off and within weeks his tactic was proven right.

### The Jackdaw
In the film *The Battle of Britain* (1969) the actor Christopher Plummer and his 'wife', played by Susannah York, have a rendezvous, which quickly develops into a bit of a tiff, in the Jackdaw Inn. This is a real pub in the village of Denton, about 9 miles south of Canterbury, and is still serving pints today.

But there is just one problem. The original name of the pub was the Red Lion and it was still known by this name at the time of the Battle of Britain. It did not become the Jackdaw until 1964.

### Hitler's invasion plan
This essentially consisted of three stages:

Sending probing attacks against the south coast and attack shipping in the Channel. This would deprive England of vital supplies and effectively impose a blockade at the same time as testing the RAF's capability to withstand Luftwaffe attacks.

Destroying as many of Fighter Command's planes as possible, in the air and while still on the ground, and put the

*The Jackdaw Inn near Canterbury as it looks today.*

airfields in the south out of action. This would necessitate fighters flying from the northern sectors to defend Kent and they would be at the limit of their combat range.

Dropping paratroops in Kent and Sussex to cause havoc inland as the Kriegsmarine and Wehrmacht (the German navy and army) launched an invasion around Dover.

What this meant in effect was that in the summer of 1940 the RAF and the Luftwaffe were engaged in a life or death struggle which came to be known as the Battle of Britain. And it was fought mainly in the skies over Kent.

## The Main Players on the German side

**Reichsmarschal Hermann Goering (1893–1946).** Commander-in-Chief of the Luftwaffe. An overweight glutton of a man and drug-addict he liked all the good things in life and enjoyed the trappings of power. Born in Bavaria he was an infantryman in the First World War but transferred to the fledgling Luftwaffe.

Goering was a gifted pilot and by the end of the war was credited with having shot down twenty-two enemy aircraft. He was a bit of an overgrown kid who loved jewellery, a life of luxury and spent time playing with his model train set when he should have been paying attention to the war. He was captured by the Allies in 1945, found guilty of war crimes but swallowed a cyanide capsule before the death sentence could be carried out.

**Generalfeldmarschall Albert Kesselring (1885–1960).** Commander of Luftflotte (Air Fleet) II. Another Bavarian who served in the First World War but he was in the artillery. His transfer to the Luftwaffe did not happen until 1933, but he proved to be a very able airman and showed great qualities of leadership. He was involved in the air campaigns in Poland, the Netherlands and Norway. His outstanding abilities did not go unnoticed and he was given command of Luftflotte II, the 'air fleet' mainly involved in the Battle of Britain. This time his military prowess was insufficient to carry the day, but he survived the wrath of Hitler and Goering to fight alongside Rommel in North Africa and then in Italy. He was tried at a special court in Venice, found guilty and sentenced to death. But the death sentence was commuted to five years in prison and he was released in 1952. He died in West Germany in July 1960.

**Generalfeldmarschall Hugo Sperrle (1885–1953).** The archetypal deferential soldier who would slavishly carry out a senior officer's orders, Sperrle too was a veteran of the First World War. He rose rapidly through the ranks and, during the Spanish Civil War, commanded the Condor Legion when it carried out the cowardly and shameless bombing of Guernica. He often did not see eye to eye with Goering, who frequently dismissed what in fact was sound advice. In particular Sperrle realised that the RAF would soon recover its Battle of Britain losses and argued against Goering's change of tactics to bombing British towns and cities. He wanted the RAF totally annihilated before any further steps were taken in the progress of the war.

Hugo Sperrle was captured by the Allies at the end of the war and put on trial. He was found not guilty of war crimes and lived to see at least a little of the aftermath of the war he had prosecuted so assiduously. He died in Munich in 1953.

## *The Main Players on the British side*

**Air Chief Marshal Sir Cyril Newall, Chief of the Air Staff (1886–1963).** The son of an army officer, Cyril Newall was born in India. He was later educated in England and, after deciding on an army career, was accepted into Sandhurst. On graduation his first posting was with the Royal Warwickshire regiment and he served on the North-West Frontier. In 1911, while enjoying a spot of leave, he took flying lessons and got the bug. When the First World War broke out he transferred to the embryonic Royal Flying Corps. His ability and natural flair were soon recognised and promotion was rapid. After the war he stayed in uniform and held several senior posts and was instrumental in the growth and development of the RAF. In 1937 he was appointed Chief of the Air Staff and immediately initiated a programme of expansion of Britain's bomber force. But as war loomed, he became convinced of the necessity for a viable fighter force and insisted on keeping the planes on British soil rather than deploying them in France. As things turned out this proved to be remarkably prescient; if the planes had been sent to France they would almost certainly have been destroyed at Dunkirk. In October 1940, when it was clear that the threat of invasion had passed, for the time being at least, Sir Cyril Newall retired. Churchill invited him to accept the post of Governor General of New Zealand and he accepted. He died in 1963.

**Air Chief Marshal Sir Hugh Dowding, Commander-in-Chief Fighter Command (1882–1970).** Born in Moffat, Scotland, Hugh Dowding was educated at Winchester School and the Royal Military Academy, Woolwich. He served his country abroad as an army officer but, like Cyril Newall, was smitten with the flying bug and joined the Royal Flying Corps in 1913. He saw action at the Somme, but was posted back to the UK to run a military training establishment at Salisbury. Between the wars he became convinced that fighters, not bombers, were required for the defence of the realm and he was largely responsible for commissioning the large-scale production of the Spitfire and Hurricane in the inter-war years. For all his ability (and he was arguably the man mostly responsible for the RAF victory in 1940) he could be prickly and difficult to get on with. He was not without enemies in the Air

Ministry, and those who wished to see him replaced were never slow to remind people of Dowding's eccentric interests: he was a vegetarian, interested in spiritualism, ghosts and, so it is reported, was a firm believer in the existence of fairies. He retired from the RAF in 1942 and after his death in 1970 his ashes were laid to rest in Westminster Abbey.

**Air Vice-Marshal Sir Keith Rodney Park, Air Officer Commanding 11 Group (1892–1975).** A New Zealander by birth but of Scottish descent, Park saw active service in the First World War in Gallipoli and at the Somme. At one point he was blown off his horse by a German shell and pronounced unfit for combat. After a period of convalescence in England he was accepted into the Royal Flying Corps in 1917, and given command of his first squadron a year later. After the war he retained his commission and worked his way up to senior positions within Fighter Command taking over as commander of 11 Group, the organisation responsible for the defence of London and the south-east, in 1940. He was still in post during the Battle of Britain and displayed remarkable nerve and imperturbability in the face of the Luftwaffe onslaught. However, like his co-warrior Dowding, soon after the battle he

*A replica of a Hawker Hurricane on view at the Battle of Britain memorial at Capel-le-Ferne, near Dover.*

was the victim of chicanery and manoeuvring, and relieved of his post. But at least he retained his commission until the end of the war. He died in New Zealand in 1975.

## MISS SHILLING'S ORIFICE

The Spitfire and Hurricane were excellent aircraft but the early version of their engine did have one drawback: it tended to flood and cut out under certain conditions and at critical moments. The solution, however, was very simple: a small washer was placed in the carburettor which restricted the flow of fuel so that just enough entered the engine but no more. The inventor was a young engineer, a certain Miss Beatrice 'Tilly' Shilling. Officially the device was referred to as an 'RAE (Royal Airforce Establishment) restrictor', but the airmen who flew the planes preferred to call it 'Miss Shilling's Orifice' or 'The Tilly Orifice'.

## THE BATTLE

We knew they were coming, but were not sure when. Then, when the enemy finally made his move in early August, it soon became clear that his intention was to deliver a knockout blow. The Luftwaffe commanders were confident that Britain would be a push-over just as Poland, France, Belgium and Holland had been but they were in for something of a surprise. Their previous adversaries had been massively out-gunned by overwhelming German forces and had crumpled in the face of their *Blitzkrieg* ('lightning war') tactics. The RAF, on the other hand, offered a stiffer challenge that was to prove truly gladiatorial.

August and September 1940 were the months during which the fate of the nation hung in the balance. The air war started on 8 August when shipping in the English Channel was attacked by the Luftwaffe and two convoys were mauled by enemy aircraft around the Isle of Wight and Bournemouth. On the 12th it was Kent's turn when over 100 aircraft flew across the Channel and attacked Dover in eleven waves. On the same day over 150 planes caused serious damage in Portsmouth and again on the Isle of

Wight. Following these attacks, on 13 and 15 August, Portsmouth was again hit, now with between 300 and 400 enemy bombers.

But the Germans were not having it all their own way. They lost 182 aircraft on 12 August alone and Goering was forced back to the drawing board. He realised that, contrary to his expectations, the RAF was not a spent force. He further reasoned that, if the RAF continued to fight in such a spirited way, his Luftwaffe would never be able to achieve the air superiority which he had personally promised the Führer. He had no option but to attack RAF fighter airfields and thus ordered his flyers to bomb those at Dover, Deal, Hawkinge, Lympne, Kenley, Biggin Hill as well as Martlesham in Suffolk and Middle Wallop in Hampshire. Once again, these attacks inflicted damage but at a cost and by 15 August the Luftwaffe had lost a total of 472 planes.

Perhaps in desperation the Luftwaffe now launched over 300 aircraft against Rochester, Kenley, Croydon, Biggin Hill, Manston, West Malling, Gosport (Hampshire), Northolt (London) and Tangmere (West Sussex) between 16 and 18 August. But these attacks alone (as it was claimed at the time) cost the enemy 245 planes. This loss rate could not be sustained, and the Germans knew it.

At this point in the war Goering stood his pilots down for a period of rest and recuperation while he considered what to do next. He continued sending the odd bomber and reconnaissance plane over the Channel but even this cost him dearly: thirty-nine aircraft were shot down in a period of five days.

When the bombers were next seen over Kent there was a noticeable change in their tactics. They no longer concentrated on the coastal areas but had inland airfields and aircraft factories in their sights. They also, obviously appreciating the prowess of the RAF Spitfire and Hurricane pilots, altered their numbers ratio: there were fewer bombers and more accompanying fighters in each formation. On 30 and 31 August 800 aircraft made a concerted effort to destroy, or at least put out of action, airfields at Kenley, North Weald, Hornchurch, Lympne, Detling, Duxford, Northolt and Biggin Hill. And things did not get any better in the first weeks of September; wave after wave of bombers came over to destroy men and machines in the south-east. But again, their raids were not without loss and in this

*The Battle of Britain Memorial. From the air the propeller-shaped layout of the memorial can be clearly seen.*

phase of the operation it was claimed that over 500 German aircraft were destroyed.

If one day, out of the eighty-four of relentless attacks, has to be selected as the climax of the battle, the only candidate for selection has to be Sunday 15 September. Beginning at 11.30 a.m. wave after wave of Dorniers and their escort of Me 109s came over the Channel and attacked targets around Ramsgate, Dover, Folkestone and close to Dungeness. Five squadrons of Spitfires flew out to intercept them in an arena stretching from Dungeness to Maidstone and Canterbury to Dover. The first attack was in two waves: the first consisted of 100 aircraft and the second 150. Some planes were shot down by the RAF but reports also claim that many of them simply turned and fled without releasing any of their bombs. On the other hand, one or two planes managed to penetrate as far as London and two heavy bombs were dropped on Buckingham Palace, although neither of them exploded. Of the total 250 planes, 60 were either destroyed or damaged. At two o'clock in the afternoon another attack came over and the pattern was repeated: flying over the coast near Dover 150 planes in the first wave were followed by 100 in the second. Twenty-one RAF squadrons were scrambled and the dogfights began. Ninety-seven enemy aircraft were destroyed in the afternoon alone as compared with RAF losses of twenty-five for the whole day, with fourteen pilots rescued.

By the end of the day it was clear that the Germans were not going to win and their dream of gaining air superiority proved as insubstantial as a wisp of Churchill's cigar smoke. The war was not yet over, but Hitler and his Luftwaffe generals had been stopped in their tracks and had been given their comeuppance by the boys of the RAF. Goering now had to do some serious rethinking as his prediction that Britain would be defeated within a couple of weeks was shown up for the fantasy it was; in the skies above Kent his dream had turned into a nightmare.

## CONCRETE RADAR?

During the 1920s the RAF experimented with huge concrete dishes intended to act in much the same way as radar did in the late 1930s. Basically they were concave structures designed to detect the sounds produced by approaching aircraft. They worked reasonably well in the days when planes flew at a relatively slow speed, but as soon as the faster ones came along these 'acoustic mirrors', as they were called, proved virtually useless and were just abandoned to the elements.

Survivors of the experiment can still be seen at the now disused RAF establishment at Denge, near Dungeness. There are three 'mirrors' of varying sizes: a 200ft curved wall, a 30ft circular dish and a 20ft circular dish.

# 9

# TRAINS

Kent is well endowed with one particular mode of transport – trains. The county is well served with the normal passenger trains that ply between places such as Dover, Ramsgate, Folkestone, Canterbury and London, etc., but it also enjoys the services of other trains which are unique to Kent: Eurostar and the Shuttle, the Kent stretch of what is usually referred to as the Orient Express and the Romney, Hythe & Dymchurch Railway.

## THE ROMNEY, HYTHE & DYMCHURCH RAILWAY

Once upon a time (actually, in about 1920) a couple of dreamers had this wonderful idea: let's build a small-scale railway in Kent. The two dreamers were a millionaire ex-army officer, Captain J.E. Howey, and Count Louis Zborowski, an extremely wealthy landowner and racing car fanatic from Bridge, near Canterbury. As neither was the type to let dreams remain dreams they went ahead and ordered two engines to be built which could run on a small gauge track. Unfortunately, the count's part in the scheme came to a sudden end when he was killed taking part in the Italian Grand Prix. This meant that the ex-army officer, undeterred by the death of his friend and fellow railway enthusiast, went ahead with the plans and decided that the most suitable place for his train would be Romney Marsh. On 16 July 1927 his wish was fulfilled and a small scale steam engine (christened *Hercules*) made the inaugural journey pulling a full complement of carriages from Hythe to the then terminus at New Romney. However, Captain Howey was not satisfied – the 8 miles or so of track was not enough for him, and he set about planning how best to extend his creation. The result was that in 1928 the line had been extended to Dungeness and travellers could now travel on the smallest passenger railway in the world all the way from Hythe to Dungeness, a distance of 13½ miles.

The railway proved to be a great success. Within no time at all it was a popular tourist attraction and it has remained so right up to the present. But there is a commercial side to the venture as well: it was and is used as a regular passenger and freight service serving the people who live on the marsh. And for many children who live in isolated places it is the only way of getting to school.

But when the war came there were big changes. The train was taken over by Somerset Light Infantry and converted into an armoured train. Its main role now was to transport troops and to offer some resistance should enemy troops attempt to cross Romney Marsh. Later on it was also used to defend a pipeline laid under the Channel to keep the troops supplied with fuel after the D-Day landings in France.

When the war was over and things started getting back to normal it was decided that the RH&DR should be 'demobbed' and returned to its civilian role. The line was reopened to the public in two stages: the stretch between Hythe and New Romney in 1946 and between New Romney and Dungeness in 1947. But the effects of the war were still being felt and what had originally been a two-track railway was forced to become single-track as the necessary raw materials were still hard to come by. Nevertheless, its return was a godsend for the travelling people of the marsh who could now enjoy some pre-war convenience and comfort. When the American film stars Laurel and Hardy cut the ribbon at the reopening ceremony, the future for many looked a little brighter than it had done for seven long years.

## The technical stuff

| Type | light railway |
| --- | --- |
| Line length | 13½ miles |
| Gauge | 1ft 3in |
| Locomotives | *Green Goddess* (steam), built 1925 |
| | *Northern Chief* (steam), built 1925 |
| | *Southern Maid* (steam), built 1926 |
| | *The Bug* (steam), built 1926 |
| | *Hercules* (steam), built 1927 |
| | *Samson* (steam), built 1927 |
| | *Typhoon* (steam), built 1927 |
| | *Hurricane* (steam), built 1927 |
| | *Winston Churchill* (steam), built 1931 |
| | *Dr Syn* (steam), built 1931 |
| | *Black Prince* (steam), built 1937 |
| | *John Southland* (diesel mechanical), built 1983 |
| | *Captain Howey* (diesel mechanical), built 1989 |

## The Numbers Game

The locomotives on the RH&DR are all numbered and range from 1 to 14. But there are only 13 locomotives. The reason for the anomaly is that it was considered unlucky to have a number 13, so there isn't one.

## . . . and some trivia

The locomotive named *Black Prince* was built in Germany and was originally called *Fliesiges Lieschen* or Busy Lizzie.

The *John Southland* is named after a local resident who left a bequest to be used for educational purposes in 1610. The locomotive of the name was sent on loan to the Liverpool Garden Festival in 1990.

Every year the trains carry a total of more than 100,000 passengers.

Based on track gauge, the RH&DR was officially recognised between 1926 and 1978 as being the smallest public railway in the world. The honour now goes to the Wells and Walsingham Light Railway in Norfolk.

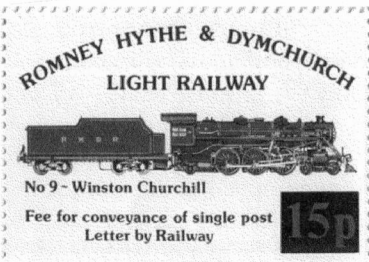

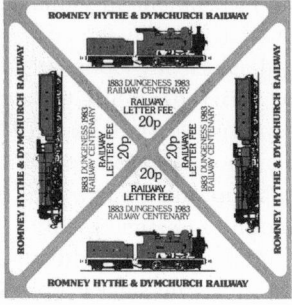

*Postage stamps of the RH&DR.*

The RH&DR operates a postal service under licence from the Royal Mail and, in the 1970s, was even permitted to issue its own stamps.

## THE ORIENT EXPRESS

Romance, drama, spies and Agatha Christie – these are just some of the words that come to mind at the mere mention of the 'Orient Express'. But the sad fact is that the train we refer to as the Orient Express has not existed for years. Even the film *Murder on the Orient Express* is something of a misnomer and, had a concern for accuracy been in the mind of the director, should have been called *Murder on the Simplon-Orient Express*. The reason for this is quite simple: the train service has gone through many transformations since its regular passenger service opened in June 1883, and by the time of the famous fictional murder the service had been renamed the 'Simplon–Orient Express'.

The 'Orient Express' was the brainchild of a Belgian, Monsieur Georges Nagelmackers, who had been impressed by the Pullman service he had seen in the USA and wanted to offer European travellers a similar mode of travel which combined efficiency with comfort and luxury. The test run took place in 1882 when guests were invited to join the train in Paris and relax, wine and dine as it sped through beautiful European countryside on its way to Vienna. The first scheduled passenger journey took place in June 1883 and over the following months the line was being continually extended until by 1885 a regular passenger service was offered from Paris to Istanbul on the Black Sea.

Any travellers from Britain who wanted to avail themselves of this magnificent example of modern transport had to make their own way to Paris before they could join the train. This meant that they had to get from London Victoria to Dover, catch the steamer to Calais and then find their way to the train and settle down for the long journey to Paris. And this was the situation until 1936.

In 1936 it was decided to make the British, if not part of the French railway system, then at least a very close working partner. Now well-to-do travellers (it was never a cheap service!) could make themselves comfortable in their compartments in London and prepare for a long journey through Europe via Dover and Dunkirk. When it arrived in Dover the train was driven straight onto a ferry which took it and the passengers over the English Channel. However, the social differences were still observed:

First-class passengers stayed in their compartments all the way to their destination. When the train arrived on the French side of the Channel the First Class carriages were joined on to French trains

Second-class passengers stayed on the train until it arrived in France but then had to make their own way off the boat and find the connecting SNCF train to take them on their way

The service was suspended at the outbreak of war in 1939 and did not resume until 1947, but its popularity never matched that of its heyday in the 1920s and '30s and as soon as the possibility of a tunnel under the English Channel began to be discussed, the 'Orient Express' was doomed. It struggled on, but by 2009 it was dead. The Shuttle and Eurostar were a reality, as were cheap air fares, and luxury travel could no longer compete.

But all was not entirely lost for those who still wanted to travel in some style. In 1982 private enterprise resurrected the age of glamour, intrigue and mystery by establishing a service from London to Venice. Using the luxurious carriages of the 1920s and '30s a new service, the 'Venice–Simplon Orient Express', was now up and running and offering modern travellers the opportunity to sample some of the grace and luxury of a bygone age. Once again it was and is possible to travel through Kent and then through Europe while sampling some on-board haute-cuisine and fine wines. However, there is a slight compromise with the opposition here: travellers are taken from London on the British Pullman train as far as Folkestone where they are then taken by bus onto the Shuttle train for the half-hour journey under the Channel. Once in Calais the genuine 'Venice–Simplon Orient Express' train is waiting to take then on to their destination.

But such travel is not for the financially squeamish: a return ticket from London to Venice costs something in the region of £2,530 (2011 price) and that does not include the cost of a hotel in Venice. The service runs from March to November and once a year the company runs a through service all the way from London to Istanbul for the benefit of the seriously romantic traveller.

### . . . and some trivia

Agatha Christie wrote *Murder on the Orient Express* in the Hotel Pera Palas in Istanbul, one of the train's original destinations.

The train featured in Ian Fleming's *From Russia with Love* and in the film version starring Sean Connery.

There is a Turkish band which plays a combination of electronic music and traditional Turkish music who call themselves The Orient Expressions.

# THE CHANNEL TUNNEL

On 1 December 1990 an event took place deep beneath the waters of the English Channel which reversed the course of history. England, once joined to the Continent, had been an island for the last 8,000 years but when Graham Fagg, digging from the English side, and Phillippe Cozette, digging from France, tore away the last clod of earth separating the two, England and France were once again joined together in what so far has proved to be holy matrimony.

Men had dreamed of constructing a tunnel beneath the English Channel for centuries as it was obvious to all that travel between England and the rest of Europe would be a lot easier if it were not for the stormy and unpredictable waters that separated the two. On the other hand, the Channel had long proved to be an effective bastion against invaders and, when the venture was mooted in the 1980s, the implications for the defence of the realm were a serious consideration. But the doubts were swept aside and the costly dream of riding beneath the waves became a reality in a matter of just a few years.

Mr Fagg and Monsieur Cozette finally brought England's isolation to an end, but there was a lot more work to be done before Europe could boast that it had 'a chunnel', as the Channel Tunnel was referred to.

## The Channel Tunnel Timeline

**1802:** The French engineer Albert Matthieu came up with the totally impracticable idea of digging a tunnel which could never have got off the drawing board. His idea was to eventually have horse-drawn carriages driving over a wooden road through a tunnel lit by candles. He had no idea how to cope with the problems of ventilation and only the barest idea of the technical problems he might encounter once the drilling commenced. Napoleon was briefly attracted to the idea for military purposes but the idea was soon shelved.

**1830s:** Another French engineer, Aimé Thomé de Gamond carried out a detailed geological and hydrographical survey of the area and arrived at the conclusion that, from a technical point of view, a tunnel beneath the Channel was perfectly feasible.

**1856:** Gamond presented his proposals to Napoleon III. In their revised form, based on the technical information his survey had produced, his plans included building an internationally administered half-way station on the Varne sandbank (just over 5 miles long and situated in the Dover Strait, 9 miles south of Dover). Shafts were to be sunk from the sandbank to ventilate the tunnel beneath where a single gas-lit tunnel would ferry steam trains and their passengers between Dover and Cap Gris Nez, south of Calais.

**1865:** An official Anglo-French working group was set up to make a feasibility study for a Channel tunnel.

**1881:** Digging started. On the English side a 7ft diameter boring machine burrowed a 6ft-long pilot tunnel at Shakespeare's Cliff near Dover and on the French side a similar machine bored a tunnel over 5,000ft long from Sangatte, near Calais. Everything was going to plan and no difficulties were encountered. Within a year almost half a mile of tunnel had been hollowed out and everybody expected the job to be completed in five years.

**1883:** Digging stopped. Certain people in Britain got cold feet and decided that a tunnel, after all, was not a good idea. The press and many politicians revived the old fears about invading armies pouring through a tunnel and securing a bridgehead in Kent.

This, for the time being, was the end of the matter. Nobody broached the subject again, although a few voices did express a certain regret at the time of the First World War that the project had been abandoned. The generals now realised that a tunnel would have made it a lot easier to get troops to the front and supply those who were already there. But it was too late; the decisions had been taken and the powers that be just had to live with them. The idea for a tunnel under the Channel was not resurrected until the 1970s.

**1973:** Edward Heath took Britain into the Europe Union (then known as the Common Market) and the idea of a tunnel began to make sense again.

**1974:** Officials from France and Britain got together again to see if they could make a final determined attempt at getting the project off the ground and get the tunnel built. Common sense dictated that it would be a good idea, and the military implications were largely irrelevant. In an age of air power and nuclear weapons the argument that a tunnel would make Britain more vulnerable now carried far less weight.

**1975:** To the chagrin of the French, Britain pulled out of discussions. The then Prime Minister, Harold Wilson, was wrestling with serious economic problems and simply could not face the prospect of dragging the country even further into debt. A massively expensive project such as the Channel Tunnel would have been an enormous drain on the country's already depleted coffers. Also, at the time there was a considerable body of opinion which argued that we should pull out of the Common Market, and this could have made all cooperation with the French government very difficult. A joint tunnel enterprise would have been an additional complication.

**1986:** But Britain did not leave the Common Market, and by the 1980s the Labour government had been replaced by Margaret Thatcher and her ruthless brand of Conservatism. Despite the fact that Mrs Thatcher, as the country's new Prime Minister, staunchly protected Britain's independence within Europe, she liked the idea of a Channel tunnel, and if she liked an idea nothing was allowed to prevent it becoming a reality. When she took office in 1979 she let it be known that she was not against the tunnel concept, provided it was financed privately. Discussions and negotiations went on quietly behind the scenes and a tentative agreement was reached. Then, in 1986, the formal agreement was signed between the French and British governments in Canterbury and the Channel Tunnel project was given the green light.

**1988:** Tunnelling began in June in the Pas-de-Calais region of France.

**1988:** Tunnelling began in December in Cheriton, near Folkestone.

**1990:** The tunnel from France and the tunnel from Britain met in the middle of the Channel and Britain ceased to be an island.

**1994:** The tunnel was formally opened in May by the French President, Monsieur François Mitterand, and Queen Elizabeth. Within a couple of months passenger and freight services were running regularly through the 'Chunnel'.

## The technical stuff

| | |
|---|---|
| Route: | Folkestone to Coquelles, Pas-de-Calais |
| Distance: | 31.3 miles |
| No. of tracks: | two single track tunnels plus one central service tunnel |
| Gauge | 4ft 8½ in |
| Undersea section: | 23½ miles |
| Deepest point | 250ft |
| Max. train speed: | 186mph |
| Journey time | London–Paris 2hrs 15mins |
| | London–Brussels 1hr 51mins |
| No. of trains: | 38 |
| Max no. of passengers: | 750 |

All passenger services are operated by Eurostar operating out of London St Pancras. Cars use the Shuttle, a drive-on – drive-off service operating from Folkestone to Calais.

## . . . and some trivia

The American Society of Civil Engineers has declared the Channel Tunnel one of the Seven Wonders of the Modern World.

Eurostar did not post its first net profits until 1999. In 1995 its losses totalled £925,000,000.

During the first few months after work began, ten workers were killed in industrial accidents on the site.

Many thought the Channel Tunnel would sound the death knell for the ferries, but by cutting the number of routes and building improved 'super' ferries they have survived.

The original projected cost of the tunnel was enormous, but even this figure paled into insignificance when the final costs were worked out: they were 80 per cent higher than originally thought.

When the construction work was at its height no fewer than 15,000 people were employed on the project.

The forecast of the number of passengers expected to use the Chunnel have never been met. The greatest number to use the service in any one year was 18.4 million in 1998.

The earth dug out of the ground once boring began was transported to a site just outside Dover to create a whole new country park known as Samphire Hoe. The spoil was landscaped so that now it just looks like an extension to the white cliffs of Dover.

In October 2010 it was announced that Eurostar intend to introduce new trains to improve passenger capacity and overall performance. The new trains will carry a maximum of 900 passengers at 200mph.

# 10

# CHALLENGE OF THE CHANNEL

The English Channel has always been a temptation. At its narrowest point it is just the right distance to make men wonder if they can fly across it, swim across it or sail across it by other than conventional means. France sits temptingly just visible on the horizon and quite brazenly calls out to both men and women on the other side like a siren, daring them to risk life and limb to cross the water under their own steam for no other reason than to be able to say 'I did it'. Some have gained financially from accepting the challenge, but almost without exception the promise of money has been merely an additional incentive; the real goad is always a sense of adventure and a deep-seated psychological urge to prove that the impossible is nothing more than an obstacle that has not yet been overcome.

## THE SWIMMERS

We have no idea how many people tried to swim across the English Channel before official records were kept, but we do know that there have been at least 1,000 successful attempts since the craze took off in the latter half of the nineteenth century. These include:

**25 August 1875:** A ship's captain in the Merchant Navy, **Matthew Webb** (1848–83), successfully swam the Channel at his second attempt. He swam from Dover to Calais in 21hrs 45 mins and became a national hero overnight. He first got the idea for the swim when a sailor on a ship he was sailing on fell overboard.

Webb dived in and tried to save the man and, although the attempt was unsuccessful and the man drowned, Webb was fired with the idea to become a professional swimmer.

**6 September 1911: Thomas William Burgess** (1872–1950) was able to duplicate Webb's success, but only at the sixteenth time of trying. He had moved to France some time around 1889 when he was offered the job of managing the French branch of a company specialising in producing tyres for the burgeoning car industry. His eventually successful Channel swim took him 22hrs 35mins.

**5 August 1923: Henry Sullivan** (b. 1893), the son of a Massachusetts businessman, managed to swim from Dover to Calais in 27hrs 25mins. The remarkable thing about this swim was not the time (Sullivan was actually slower than Webb and Burgess) but the distance he covered. As the crow flies the distance from Dover to Calais is just less than 23 miles, but because of the currents and the choppy conditions in the Channel on the day of his attempt, he actually covered something like 56 miles. So, although he took five or six hours more than his predecessors, he covered more than twice the distance.

**13 August 1923:** The Argentinian, **Enrique Tirabocchi** (aka Enrico Tiraboschi), completed the swim in what turned out to be a record time: 16hrs 33mins. However, there are those who detract from his achievement because he swam from France to England which, because of the tides etc. is supposed to be a much easier way of completing the swim.

**9 September 1923:** The American **Charles Toth** completed the swim in 16hrs 40mins. Unfortunately, he was not eligible for the *Daily Sketch* prize of £1,000 because he missed the expiry date by which, according to the rules, all swims had to be completed, by just two days. His predecessors, Tirabocchi and Sullivan both satisfied the conditions and were presented with the cheques as soon as they reached terra firma.

**6 August 1926: Gertrude Ederle** (1905–2003) was the first woman to complete the swim. An American champion swimmer she was trained by Thomas William Burgess when she decided that she was going to make an attempt on the English Channel. She opted for the France–UK route and completed the swim from Cap Gris Nez to Kingsdown in Kent in 14hrs 39mins. Unbelievably, as she pulled herself exhausted and bedraggled out of the water on the Kent beach the first person she met was a British Immigration official asking to see her passport! Another account of this story says that the encounter took place on a tugboat before the swimmer was allowed ashore.

**28 August 1926: Amelia Gade Corson** was born in Copenhagen, Denmark, in about 1899. Very little is known of her early life and even the year of her birth is not known for certain. It is known, however, that she moved to the United States in 1919 and took up swimming as a hobby. One of her aquatic achievements was to swim around Manhattan Island, a distance of 42 miles, in a time of 16hrs. Her swim across the Channel was from Cap Gris Nez to Dover and she completed the crossing in 15hrs 29mins. In the world of 'firsts' she can rightly claim to be the first mother to complete the Channel swim.

**August 1927: Edward H. Temme** became the first man to swim the Channel in both directions, although not at one go! In August 1927 he swam from France to England and then, in August 1934, he completed the swim again but this time from England to France.

**8 August 1950: Florence May Chadwick** (1918–95), the daughter of a San Diego policeman, was the first woman to swim the Channel both ways. She first completed the swim from Cap Gris Nez to Dover in August 1950 in a time of 13hrs 20mins and then, in August 1951 swam from Dover to Sangatte, near Calais, in 16hrs 22mins.

**21 September 1961:** The Argentinian **Antonio Abertondo** (1918–78) achieved one of the greatest feats in the history of Channel swimming: he was the first man to swim both ways without stopping. He was a veteran Channel swimmer, having successfully completed the crossing in 1950, 1951 and 1954 and was no doubt looking for something more of a challenge. He decided to attempt what most people thought was totally beyond human endurance and completed the round trip in 43hrs 10mins.

**1981: Jon Erikson** (b. 1955), a PE teacher from America, was the first of only three people to swim the Channel three ways. His time in 1981 was 38hrs 27mins. This was not his first time in the Channel as he completed the two-way crossing in 1975 in a time of 30hrs and then repeated the feat in 1979 in 22hrs 16mins. He completed no fewer than eleven cross-Channel swims between 1969 and 1981.

**Alison Streeter** (b. 1964) is an amazing athlete. She gave up her job as a London currency trader to devote her time and energy to swimming and her achievements in the water are just incredible. She has swum the Channel forty-three times (a world record) and is, not surprisingly, known as 'the Queen of the Channel'. She also (a) has completed a triple crossing (b) has swum the Channel seven times in one year (c) holds the record for the France–England crossing with a time of 8hrs 48mins and (d) in 1990 swam the Channel three ways non-stop in 34hrs 40mins. She was awarded a well-deserved MBE in 1991.

**4 July 2006: David Walliams,** the TV personality and star of *Little Britain*, swam the English Channel and so raised £1,000,000 for charity.

**July 2010:** The longest time for a cross-Channel swim was recorded by Jackie Cobell, a mother of two from Five Oak Green near Tonbridge. She set out from Dover intending to complete the crossing in an average time but took far longer. The tides in the Channel took her way off course and instead of the planned 23 miles or thereabouts she swam an amazing 65 miles, arriving in Calais after a swim lasting 28hrs 44mins.

**August 2007:** The Bulgarian champion swimmer, **Petar Stoychev** (b. 1976) took the crown for the fastest person to swim the Channel. He covered the distance from Dover to Cap Gris Nez in 6hrs 57mins.

**18 September 2010:** The Frenchman **Philippe Croizon** swam from Folkestone to Cap Gris Nez in 14hrs, which is about average. But it is only 'average' until we remember that forty-two-year-old Monsieur Croizon has no arms or legs! He had to have his limbs amputated after being electrocuted in 1994 but, after an understandable period of despair, learned to live with his disability and get used to living with prosthetic arms and legs. And it was with these same artificial arms and legs that he propelled himself across the Channel to accomplish what can only be described as a feat of remarkable courage and determination.

## . . . and some trivia

Only about 7 per cent of attempts to swim the Channel end in success.

Among long-distance swimmers the English Channel is regarded as the Mount Everest of swims.

The oldest person to complete the swim is George Brunstad. He completed the crossing in August 2004 when he was 70 years and 4 days old. His swim time was 15hrs 59mins.

The youngest person to swim the Channel is Thomas Gregory who was 11 years 11months old when he completed the crossing in 1988.

Long-distance swimmers usually maintain a rate of 60 or 70 strokes per minute.

One of the major obstacles with which swimmers have to deal in the English Channel are shoals of jellyfish.

## THE BALLOONISTS

The first balloon crossed the Channel in the eighteenth century and then, once it had been proven that balloons could possibly offer travellers another mode of transport, the whole idea seemed to 'take off', as it were.

**February 1784:** An unmanned balloon released from Sandwich rose gracefully into the air and then drifted eastwards until it came to earth in Flanders, some 75 miles away.

**January 1785:** A Mr Blanchard and a Dr Jeffries ascended from Dover Castle and landed in northern France after something of a hair-raising flight over the English Channel. The main problem seems to have been maintaining altitude and they were forced to throw just about everything overboard in an attempt to gain height. Several times it looked as if the venture could end in disaster (or, at the very least, an ignominious ditching). Fortunately they eventually landed safely, if very shaken by the experience.

**March 1882:** A Mr Simmons and a Colonel Brine set off from somewhere near Canterbury. At first everything seemed to be going according to plan. The weather was excellent and the visibility unbelievably good. But a few miles into the flight things turned dramatically worse and the gallant adventurers were blown way off course and, when they lost sight of land altogether, feared they were drifting into the North Sea. They had no alternative but to ditch their craft although fortunately they did come down in the English Channel and were fished out by the crew of a passing ferry.

**March 1882 (later):** Another soldier, Colonel Burnaby (1842–85), decided he would attempt to succeed where his colleague had failed. He acquired a balloon, filled it with gas in Folkestone and then had it towed all the way to Dover. The launch took place at noon and Colonel Fred Burnaby and the balloon drifted slowly above Dover and then out across the Channel, making a successful crossing and landing in Envermeau, Normandy, a few hours later. He thus became the first person to make a successful balloon crossing of the English Channel alone. Colonel Burnaby died in 1885 from wounds received on the battlefield in Sudan.

## THE AVIATORS

Man has always dreamed of being able to fly. Galileo Galilei (1564–1642) drew up elaborate plans for a flying machine and heaven alone knows how many people have thrown themselves off high buildings and mountain tops, convinced in their own minds that they would be able to emulate the birds in the sky. Not many lived to have a second go. But, after the Wright brothers' first flight on 17 December 1903, there was no looking back. And when they gave their first public demonstration of flight at a race-track near Le Mans in August 1908 among the spectators was a certain French engineer, Monsieur Louis Blériot (1872–1936), whose imagination was fired by what he saw. He began designing and building his own 'heavier-than-air' craft and then set himself the task of flying across the English Channel.

1903–6: Blériot and his colleague Gabriel Voisin ran their own company producing early aircraft. None of them was particularly successful and, in fact, some of them turned out to be positive death-traps. When the money ran out the company ceased to exist but Blériot refused to give up his dream. He designed several prototypes, but they met with nothing more than modest success.

1909: By now Blériot had figured out where he had been going wrong and, with several more near misses behind him, produced a reasonably stable and well-behaved aircraft which he called the Blériot XI. After a few trials over land he decided to attempt the Channel crossing. Just before dawn on 25 July he took off from Les Baraques, near Calais, and landed 37 minutes later in

a field near Dover. There was a considerable amount of damage
to the plane but not enough to detract from Monsieur Blériot's
achievement. He had not just flown across the Channel; he had
opened a whole new vista to mankind and his irrepressible urge
to travel.

### The technical stuff

| | |
|---|---|
| Configuration: | monoplane |
| Length: | 25ft |
| Wingspan: | 25ft 7in |
| Height: | 8ft 10in |
| Power: | 25hp, three-cylinder Anzani radial engine |
| Propeller | two-bladed, fixed-pitch |
| Average airspeed: | 40mph |

Over the Channel

| | |
|---|---|
| Altitude: | 250ft (approx) |
| Total flight: | 22 statute miles |

### . . . and some trivia

Louis Blériot made a fortune manufacturing acetylene lamps and
invented car headlamps.

His first venture into flight was his invention of a contraption
called an *ornithopter* (Greek for 'bird wing'). It never even got off
the ground, either literally or metaphorically.

He opened flying schools in Britain: one at Hendon and one at Brooklands.

The UK company Virgin Trains named one of their trains the *Louis Blériot* in honour of the pioneering aviator in 2002.

His flight across the Channel won him a £1,000 prize organised by the *Daily Mail*.

History has tended to fix her gaze on Monsieur Blériot and conveniently (or inconveniently) forget that he had his competitors. There was the Russian nobleman of French descent, **Charles de Lambert** (1865–1944), who was passionate about flying and was actually given instruction in the new science by the Wright brothers. He intended to race Blériot across the Channel but, in a practice run near the coastal town of Wissant, crashed his plane and his injuries were severe enough to ground him.

Another more serious contender was **Hubert Latham** (1883–1912). Despite his English-looking name he was a Frenchman (although his forebears were English and he did spend a year at Oxford University), congenitally fascinated by things mechanical. As his natural aptitude for engines, etc., coincided with the birth of aviation it is not surprising that he soon turned his attention to the 'daring young men in their flying machines' and decided to become one of them. He learned to fly in 1909, impressing his instructors with the rapidity with which he mastered the complicated controls; in fact, within a very short time Latham was

no longer a pupil but found himself appointed principal instructor at one of the early French flying schools.

If things had gone according to plan, Latham could easily have been the first to fly the Channel. Unfortunately a series of mishaps and blunders made him an also-ran. On 9 July 1909 he gathered his little team in Sangatte in Pas-de-Calais and began preparations for what he hoped would be a historic flight. Unfortunately the weather was against him, and it was not until 19 July that he was able to take off. Had he completed the crossing he would have beaten Blériot by six days, but he did not. A mere 8 miles into the flight his *Antionette IV* aircraft developed engine trouble and he was forced to ditch in the Channel and wait to be rescued.

The damage to the plane was so severe that another had to be despatched from the factory so that he could make a second attempt. This plane, the *Antoinette VII* was the firm's newest model and hopes of a successful flight were high. If reports of the day are to be believed what happened next is almost unbelievable. The weather was again too bad to allow flying and Latham and his arch-rival Blériot went to bed hoping for better weather the next morning. The Blériot team stayed up and, well before dawn, suddenly noticed that the meteorological conditions had improved and wakened the aviator. He flew off and was almost half-way across the Channel by the time Latham opened his eyes. He missed his chance simply because he and his team overslept!

When he did finally take off he knew he was settling for second best. But even this attempt was doomed. On 27 July he took off and had almost completed the crossing when disaster struck. Gallingly, when he was in sight of Dover and just a few minutes away from completing the crossing, his engine failed again. There was nothing he could do and he had to just sit there and watch the waters of the Channel get closer and closer. This time the plane was a write-off and he never attempted the crossing again.

## The technical stuff

| | |
|---|---|
| Configuration: | monoplane |
| Length: | 37ft 9in |
| Wingspan: | 42ft 8in |
| Height: | 9ft 10in |
| Wing area: | 538 sq ft |

| | |
|---|---|
| Gross weight: | 1,300lb |
| Max speed: | 44mph |
| Power: | one Antoinette 8V, 37kW (50hp) |

*. . . and some trivia*
Latham is credited with making the first landing on water. In fact, he just ditched.

On his gravestone in Le Havre, one of his names is recorded Louis instead of Charles. A Freudian slip?

Controversy surrounds his death. Officially he was gored by a rampaging buffalo while on an expedition in Africa. Other reports suggest he was murdered by his porters.

Despite his failure over the Channel he did manage a couple of firsts: he was the first person to fly over a city, Berlin, and was the first to hunt duck from an aeroplane.

## SOME OF THE WACKY ONES

Some people like to cross the Channel in comfort; some prefer the more adventurous means of transport and some like the downright loony. Here are some of the more unusual ways man (and in some cases, woman) has attempted to get over from Kent to France.

**Jim Potts** and **John Pilkington,** both microlight enthusiasts, decided that it might be a bit of a prank to attempt the crossing in their preferred mode of transport. They made the crossing from Dover to France on 13 September 1981. Their vehicle of choice was a Chargus Titan with a 432cc Fuji Robin trike engine and they became the first persons to fly across the Channel in a two-seater microlight machine.

**Bernard Thomas,** from Llechryd in South Wales, a life-long coracle enthusiast decided in 1974 that he would have a go at crossing the English Channel in one of his tiny craft. It took him several attempts, but on the third he crossed from St Margaret's Bay, near Dover, and touched land in France 13hrs 30mins later.

**Yves Rossy,** a Swiss adventurer who has been dubbed 'the birdman', flew across the Channel in September 2008 on a jet-pack and carbon fibre wings capable of reaching 125mph. He made the crossing in just under 10 minutes and then parachuted back to earth.

**Sir Richard Branson,** the business tycoon who is never shy about getting involved in unusual escapades, decided to have a go at crossing the Channel in a £75,000 amphibious vehicle in 2004. In the event he broke the existing record and crossed from Dover to Calais in 1hr 40mins. The vehicle he used for his attempt was a Gibbs Aquada which is capable of travelling at 100mph over land and 30mph over water.

**James Cracknell OBE,** the Olympic rower, along with surfing coach **Pete Craske** made a brave but unsuccessful attempt at crossing the Channel in September 2005 on surfboards. Everything seemed to be going well for them until they were a mere 8 miles off the French coast when they were caught in a swell and had to be rescued. But they did succeed on a second attempt a few days later, completing the crossing in 5hrs 26mins.

**Major Phil Packer MBE,** an officer in the British Army who was badly injured while serving in Iraq, decided that, despite being left paraplegic, he would row across the English Channel. He accomplished the task in February 2009, together with another adventurer, **Alastair Humphries,** and the pair raised over £150,000 for the British charity for injured servicemen and women, Help for Heroes.

**Paul Tucker,** an ex-army major, crossed the English Channel on a pedalo in 2002. He set off from Folkestone, pedalled all the way to Calais and then pedalled all the way back again.

**The Sisterhood,** as they style themselves, became the first all-ladies team to row their way across the English Channel. They accomplished their feat in a dragon boat in 2007 and the crew was meant to include Kate Middleton (the then lady-friend of Prince William) but she was forced to withdraw as there were concerns about her security.

**Campbell Holm** and **Marcel Syron** made an attempt at crossing the Channel in August 2009 in what they called a 'boatle'. This was a Heath Robinson contraption consisting of bits of foam and wood glued together and tied to 600 plastic bottles. They did all their practising for the big day on London canals and then in the sea off Brighton, but soon found out that the English Channel is not a canal! They failed.

**Christine Bleakley,** the Northern Irish television personality, undertook one of the most daring ways of attempting to cross the Channel . . . on water-skis. After months of gruelling training she set off from Dover on 12 March 2010 and, although she fell in the water eight times, became the first person ever to water-ski across the Channel. The turbulent crossing to Calais took 1hr 40mins.

**Jonathan Trappe**, a daredevil American, hit on the wacky idea of flying across the Channel dangling from nothing more than a huge bunch of kids' balloons! He set off from Ashford on 28 May 2010 at 5.00 a.m. strapped to a chair beneath dozens of helium-filled balloons and, unbelievably, made the crossing safely and landed in a bewildered Frenchman's vegetable garden just 4 hours later.

In July 2007 **Jeremy Clarkson, Richard Hammond** and **James May**, all television presenters, thought it would be a bit of a prank to 'drive' specially adapted cars across the English Channel. Unfortunately Hammond's and May's craft both sank and all three had to attempt the crossing in Jeremy Clarkson's 4x4 Nissan truck, fitted with an outboard motor and empty oil drums for added stability. Things looked a bit hairy at first as they tried to manoeuvre out of Dover harbour, but eventually they got the hang of it and came ashore near Calais some hours later.

## GOSSAMER ALBATROSS

Essentially the Gossamer Albatross was nothing more than a glorified bike! It was the invention of an American engineer, Dr Paul B. MacCready, and his design team, who had long been interested in the phenomenon of flight and how to overcome the problems associated with it. Their Gossamer Albatross involved flight in a craft powered by nothing more than human muscle, as the pilot had to sit and pedal for dear life if the craft was to remain airborne. The pedals were attached to a large, two-bladed propeller which needed 0.4hp in order to function.

When the Gossamer Albatross completed a successful crossing of the Channel on 12 June 1979 the pilot was Bryan Allen, an amateur cyclist. The journey took him 2hrs 49mins and his top speed was 18mph. For the greater part of the flight he was no more than 5ft above the water.

On 7 July 1981 a solar-powered version, known as Solar Challenger, piloted by Steve Ptacek, flew from Paris to Manston Airfield in Kent (a distance of 163 miles) in 5hrs 23 mins.

### . . . and some trivia
In 1992 the remains of a boat were discovered near Dover dating back to around 1550 BC. It appears that the original was constructed of oak planks tied together with sprigs of yew and might have been used to carry up to 12 passengers over the Channel.

When the Duke of Wellington defeated Napoleon at Waterloo, Belgium, in 1815 the news was conveyed to London by carrier pigeon which had to fly over the English Channel.

In 1910 the first passengers were taken on a flight over the Channel. An American pilot, John Bevins Moisant, made the flight taking his cat and a mechanic for company.

# ACKNOWLEDGEMENTS

There are several people whom I have to thank for their valuable assistance while I was gathering and assembling the material which became the building blocks for this book. My wife, Jean, helped me enormously with her encouragement and ingenious suggestions, but perhaps even more importantly, she prepared delicious meals for me to look forward to after a hard day's slaving over a hot keyboard. All I had to do was open the wine.

Also, I am extremely grateful to my daughter, Mrs Kirstine Borrello, whose artistic talents came to my rescue in the preparation of the line drawings. It was a part of the proceedings which caused me the greatest concern and she came to my rescue just in time, producing drawings which would have been totally beyond my limited capabilities.

I would also like to say 'thank you' to the staff of the Folkestone Library for way they coped with several of my requests for rather obscure bits of information.

Last but by no means least I would like to thank Michelle Tilling of The History Press for offering me this fascinating project.

# BIBLIOGRAPHY

*Books & Periodicals*

Ashworth, William J., 'Smugglers and the Birth of Britain's Consumer Society', *BBC History Magazine*, Vol. 11, No. 8, August 2010

Atkinson, William C., *A History of Spain and Portugal*, Penguin, 1970

Bede, *A History of the English Church and People*, Penguin Classics, 1968

Cawthorne, Bob, *The Isle of Thanet Compendium*, Scribble and Doodle Books, 2007

Doel, Fran and Geoff, *Folklore of Kent*, The History Press, 2003

*Great Writers – Exclusive Books*, WH Smith, 1992

Guilmant, Aylwin, *Kent of One Hundred Years Ago*, Alan Sutton Publishing, 1992

Harris, Paul, *Folkestone: A History and Celebration*, Ottakar's, 2004

Hindley, Geoffrey, *A Brief History of the Anglo-Saxons*, Constable & Robinson, 2006

Jessup, F.W., *A History of Kent*, Phillimore & Co., 1995

Mason, Phil, *Kent Chronicles of Catastrophe and Disaster*, Countryside Books, 2008

Morgan, Kenneth O. (ed.), *The Oxford Illustrated History of Britain*, OUP, 1989

Ousby, Ian (ed.), *The Cambridge Guide to English Literature*, CUP, 1988

Ridley, Jasper, *The Tudor Age*, Constable & Robinson, 2002

Southgate, George W., *A Textbook of Modern History 1789–1960*, J.M. Dent & Sons, 1961

Stenton, Frank, *Anglo-Saxon England*, 3rd edn, Oxford University Press, 1971

*The Battle of Britain August – October 1940. An Air Ministry Account*, His Majesty's Stationary Office, 1941

Weigall, Arthur, *Wanderings in Anglo-Saxon Britain*, Hodder & Stoughton, 1950

Whiting, Roger, *The Spanish Armada*, Sutton Publishing, 2004

Whynne-Hammond, Charles, *English Place-names Explained*, Countryside Books, 2005

## Websites

www.bbc.co.uk/history
www.raf.mod.uk/bob
www.martello-towers.co.uk
www.cinqueports.org
www.faversham.org.uk
www.villagenet.co.uk
www.historylearningsite.co.uk
www.dovermuseum.co.uk

## Other titles published by The History Press

### Front-Line Kent
MICHAEL FOLEY

ISBN 978-0-7509-4460-1

Featuring Roman forts, Martello Towers, the ambitious Royal
Military Canal, wartime airfields and underground Cold War
installations, this book is sure to be of interest to military
enthusiasts.

### Kent Murders
LINDA STRATMANN

ISBN 978-0-7509-4811-1

Among the gruesome cases featured here are the couple who were
brutally battered to death in their beds in Chislehurst and the
strange death of a young German man whose body was discovered
with one hand missing on Ramsgate beach. All manner of murder
and mystery are included here, making *Kent Murders* a must-read
for true crime enthusiasts everywhere.

### Historic Kent
A PHOTOGRAPHIC GUIDE

BEN & ZOE ANKER

ISBN 978-0-7509-4320-8

*Historic Kent* is an introduction to much of what the county
has to offer – from cathedrals and castles to coastlines and
country gardens. It is a colourful photographic journey
around the county which is sure to appeal to residents and
visitors alike.

Visit our website and discover thousands of other History Press books.

**www.thehistorypress.co.uk**